HUMANITY IN ACTION

Collected Essays and Talks by Judith S. Goldstein

Humanity in Action: Collected Essays and Talks by Judith S. Goldstein

ISBN-10: 0692208534
ISBN-13: 978-0-692-20853-3

Humanity in Action Press

To the Humanity in Action Senior Fellows

Table of Contents

Introduction

These essays share a common base of concerns about pluralism, resilience, civic engagement, resistance, democratic societies and the efforts to oppose discrimination, autocratic regimes and conflict aimed at specific minorities. The subjects are those that spring from the mission of Humanity in Action—a mission that depends upon connecting past to present and educating students and young professionals immersed in both domestic and global issues and responsibilities.

I am most grateful to the many constituencies in Humanity in Action who have encouraged the thoughts and ideas expressed in the essays and talks. I have benefited, in particular, from the fine editing skills of Antje Scheidler and Anthony Chase.

About Humanity in Action

Humanity in Action educates university students and young professionals who now form a unique international community. Through its programs and partnerships with outstanding civic and educational organizations including The New School, Humanity in Action contributes in innovative ways to advance human rights and democratic freedoms.

Humanity in Action's annual fellowship programs bring together more than 100 European and American university students and young professionals each summer in Denmark, France, Germany, Poland and the Netherlands to discuss, learn and research in international groups. Humanity in Action Fellows meet leading experts and activists to study the Holocaust and contemporary challenges to minority rights. Fellows write research-based articles and develop teaching tools to share what they learned in their programs. Humanity in Action supports all Fellows financially for the duration of their programs, allowing for the merit-based selection of diverse applicants.

Humanity in Action also provides professional development opportunities. It maintains an international network of students, young professionals, established leaders, experts and partners for which it organizes a range of educational and career opportunities, including seminars, workshops, study trips and fellowship positions at leading civic and political institutions, such as the European Parliament, U.S. Congress, and the International Criminal Tribunal for the Former Yugoslavia. These opportunities encourage emerging leaders to develop their professional abilities and introduce established leaders to the ideas of the younger generation.

Humanity in Action's network of leaders is a valuable resource to policy-makers, diplomats, educators, business leaders and civic-minded individuals and organizations. By the end of the decade, Humanity in Action will connect over 2,500 professionals working in all sectors, on a range of critical issues, in countries around the world.

Humanity in Action is a non-profit, non-partisan organization with governing and advisory Boards in Bosnia and Herzegovina, Denmark, France, Germany, the Netherlands, Poland and the United States. Humanity in Action's international headquarters is in New York City.

Major supporters of Humanity in Action have included the Ford Foundation, Mellon Foundation, the Richard and Rhoda Goldman Fund, Foundation Remembrance, Germeshausen Foundation, Hurford Foundation, the Responsibility and Future Fund (EVZ), the Dutch Ministry for Health, Welfare and Sport, United States Department of State and the Polish Foreign Ministry.

The Myth of Anne Frank

Partisan Review, Winter, 2003

For millions of people, Anne Frank's history has come to symbolize one of Europe's deadliest conflagration—a time when one nation set fire to its democratic government, ravaged countries all over the Continent, destroyed Jewish life in Eastern Europe and irreparably damaged Jewish existence in many Western European countries as well. The outlines of Anne Frank's history are clear: the escape with her family from Germany; resettlement in 1933 in Amsterdam where her father Otto Frank had a business; German occupation of The Netherlands in May, 1940; the family's flight in 1942 into hiding in the attic above Otto Frank's office; writing in her diary; betrayal and capture in August 1944; imprisonment in Westerbork, a transit camp; deportation to Auschwitz in September 1944; death in Bergen-Belsen a few weeks before liberation in March 1945; Otto Frank's return as the sole surviving member of the family; publication, in the early 1950s, of the diary found by Miep Gies after the police arrested the Franks; posthumous fame for Anne and her family.

The Diary of Anne Frank and derivative theatrical productions have made a unique impact on children and adults throughout the world. They connect the public with vulnerability, innocence and torment during the Holocaust. The writing bespeaks of courage, misery, persecution and resistance. Anne Frank has come to represent the child, in her mid-teens, struggling to maintain hope and faith in mankind, if not in her own future. The most famous quote from her diary is: "In spite of everything I still believe people are good at heart."[1] Sudden capture stopped the flow of testimony of inner thoughts.

An aura of sweet optimism and faith surrounds the *Diary*. Unfortunately, the sentiments are misapplied. Cynthia Ozick's critique is closer to the truth. She described the Diary as a "chronicle of trepidation, turmoil, alarm.... Betrayal and arrest always threaten. Anxiety and immobility rule. It is a story of fear." People know that Anne as well as her sister and mother were exterminated but for many readers Anne's story ends with the hope that "people are really good at heart." These words, I believe, are the key to understanding the conversion of her diary and personae into a

1 Ozick, Cynthia, *The New Yorker*, Oct. 6, 1997, p. 78.

redemptive myth.

Ian Buruma wrote that Anne Frank has "become a Jewish Saint Ursula, a Dutch Joan of Arc, a female Christ." He concluded: "Anne is a ready-made icon for those who have turned the Holocaust into a kind of secular religion."[2] I would take the comparisons even further. Despite the evolution of Europe's post-war secular spirit, the myth derives much of its force from a deeply ingrained Christian template. Anne's story converges into elements of Christian belief and symbolism: a Jewish child, a hidden child, a virgin, a betrayal, the Holocaust as Hell, a form of resurrection through her words, a place of pilgrimage and contact with her life, an offering of consoling, forgiving and hopeful words for those who survive her death.

The redemptive tale seems tragically simple. But the real history is complex and convoluted. It is part of a Dutch national tragedy in a country of contradictions. The German occupation exacerbated passive political and social habits and traditions that affected the individual and collective life of the Dutch. The Anne Frank legend has further blurred the history of Dutch Jews and the Dutch nation during the War. A sorting out is long overdue.

In an essay published in the early 1981, the American historian Simon Schama highlighted some of those Dutch paradoxes in regard to the Jews. Schama was writing about Rembrandt's time when Jews were welcomed in Amsterdam but also subject to restrictions in terms of occupation, membership in guilds, political rights and religious expression. In his introduction to an exhibition of Rembrandt's images of Jews in The Netherlands, Schama wrote: "The relationship of the host culture to its Jewish immigrants was... clouded with ambiguities." He continued: "Compared with other seventeenth century options, it cannot be overstressed, the Dutch Republic was a paradise of toleration and security.... And it is a mark of the extent to which they could invent an authentically Dutch-Jewish identity that many of the paradoxes and conflicts in which the community was caught reflected paradoxes and conflicts that lay within the heart of Dutch culture itself. For that compressed little power-house of wealth and ingenuity vibrated to the throb of its own contradictions."[3]

Schama described Amsterdam in the 17th century as a "relatively benevolent milieu" for Jews—one in which they could develop an identity in the Dutch context. "For its sheer regularity, the undisturbed ordinariness, with which Amsterdam Jews went about marrying; raising their young, burying their dead; cleaning their houses before Pesach; gathering together in their splendid temples for the Sabbath and the solemn feasts and fasts—that testifies most eloquently to the emergence of an authentic Dutch Jewish culture. In some ways Amsterdam, with its hectic oscillation between mass piety and mass hedonism, was an odd habitat for this Great Calming Down to occur.... Despite the golden crown on the spire of the Westerkerk, it wasn't really Jerusalem. But then it wasn't Babylon, either."[4]

---

2 Buruma, Ian, *The New York Review of Books*, Feb.19, 1998.

3 Morgenstein, Susan W. and Levine, Ruth E., *The Jews in the Age of Rembrandt*, p. 9.

4 Ibid p. 17.

Given this remarkable advance in acceptance by a European country, the Jewish population in the Netherlands continued to expand and confidently regard itself as part of the Dutch nation. In Rembrandt's time, the Jewish population was 10,000. Two centuries later, it was 140,000. By 1940, many Jews had attained high levels of prosperity, recognition and acceptance in Dutch life, although not to the degree characteristic of German Jews before the rise of Hitler. Forty per cent of the Jewish population lived in small villages, towns or cities such as The Hague. The other 60% lived in Amsterdam. A large number of them were poor. Through the 1930s, Dutch Jews focused on internal issues of assimilation, integration and the well-being of the Jewish community despite the fact that Nazi rule in Germany compelled thousands of Jews, such as Otto Frank, to seek refuge in the Netherlands.

The Dutch haven, developed with such promise since the 17th Century, appeared secure until the spring of 1940 when Germany conquered the Netherlands. The Dutch fought for five days and then capitulated. The Queen and government fled to London, established a resistance government in exile and urged the Dutch at home to oppose the Germans. The presence of thousand of Germans—administrators, police and soldiers—an acquiescent or obliging Dutch civil service, and the active support of Dutch Nazis quickly turned The Netherlands into a subject state. The government in Berlin put the Dutch under the control of Seys-Inquart, an accomplished Nazi fresh from anti-Semitic conquests in Austria. From that point on, to refer back to Schama, for the Jews Amsterdam was neither Jerusalem nor Babylon. It was hell.

“The separation of Jews from the rest of Dutch society consisted of ending their rights to property, education, work and mobility. Jews were not allowed to use the trams or bicycles, enter parks or swimming pools, go to movie houses or theaters, and use the beaches.”

It didn't take long for the Germans to differentiate Jews from other Dutch citizens through anti-Jewish decrees and administrative acts: first, the prohibition against Jewish civil servants and teachers; then, in 1941violent assaults against Jews in the Jewish Quarter in Amsterdam. The Germans insisted that the Jews form a Jewish Council to make the Jewish community respond to increasingly punitive German demands. The separation of Jews from the rest of Dutch society consisted of ending their rights to property, education, work and mobility. Jews were not allowed to use the trams or bicycles, enter parks or swimming pools, go to movie houses or theaters, and use the beaches. Schools for children were segregated, universities were closed for Jewish professors and students, Jewish musicians and actors were no longer allowed to perform. And shopping was only allowed for Jews in narrow time slots. (These were the same kinds of restrictions that the Germans imposed upon their own Jews in the 1930s.)

Initially, German policies of disenfranchisement and persecution infuriated the

Dutch. In February 1941, many Dutch launched a general strike, which closed down the docks, transportation system and industry. This great spasm of opposition to the Germans—and outrage against the treatment of the Jews—lasted three days. The punitive German response pushed the Dutch back into acquiescence and did nothing to stop the increasing physical isolation of the Jews, their economic ruination and the "razia" or roundups and deportations. Resistance flared again in the spring of 1942,when every Dutch Jew was ordered to buy and wear a yellow star with "Jood"— "Jew" written on it. Many Dutch non-Jews put on the yellow star or a yellow flower in solidarity with the Jews. It made a strong impression on Miep Gies, protector of the Frank family. "The yellow stars and yellow flowers those first few days were so common," she wrote in her book *Anne Frank Remembered*, "that our River Quarter was known as the Milky Way.... A surge of pride and solidarity swelled briefly until the Germans started cracking heads and making arrests. A threat was delivered to the population at large: anyone assisting Jews in any way would be sent to prison and possibly executed."[5]

Life for the Jews in the Netherlands ground down to a devastating pattern of anxiety and violent round ups for Jews, their protectors and those in the resistance movement. Unlike the Jews in Denmark who could escape to Sweden, the Dutch Jews had nowhere to go. Some, such as the Franks withdrew into silent hiding in buildings in the cities and countryside. They were totally dependent on their Dutch protectors who resisted the Germans by housing, feeding, clothing and caring for Jews. Of the 140,000 Jews in the Netherlands in 1940, about 20,000 went into hiding. Approximately 7,000 of them were discovered. They shared the fate of the majority of Dutch Jews: removal to the Westerbork camp and then deportation to Sobibor and Auschwitz in the East. By the time that the process was complete, 110,000 Dutch Jews had been killed.

The German occupation sorely challenged traditional Dutch relationships, attitudes and behavior built upon a seemingly strong facade of tolerance and compromise. The political and social acceptance of differences obscured the fateful gulf between tolerance, on the one hand, and disinterest and disengagement, on the other. In regard to national cohesion and separate ethnic, religious and political identities, the War tested the viability of the so-called Dutch pillar society, based upon separate realms of allegiance among Protestant, Catholic, Socialist and Liberal groups. With insidious understanding of Dutch passivity, and the narrowly focused "pillarized" affiliations—above all else, the Dutch yearning for order, the acceptance of government rules to insure that order, the obedience of civil servants to carry through ordinances of order—the Germans surgically removed the Jews out of Dutch life. And when so removed, the Jews disappeared from the realm of responsibility and moral concern of most of Dutch society.

Despite the humiliation and anxiety of occupation, only in the last year of the war did the non-Jewish Dutch—and principally those in the large Northern

5 Gies, Miep, *Anne Frank Remembered*, p. 87.

cities—suffer acutely from the depletion of goods and food, the dangers of forced labor in Germany and the desperate wait for the defeat of the Germans. It finally came on May 4, 1945 to the northern part of the country that was starved, sick and degraded. When the Germans finally surrendered, the Dutch celebrated for days in the streets. The Queen came back. "People who had been in hiding came out onto the streets," Miep Gies wrote. "Jews came out of hiding places, rubbing eyes that were unused to sunlight, their faces yellow and pinched and distrustful. Church bells rang everywhere; streamers flew.... To wake up and go through a whole day without any sense of danger was amazing."[6]

And then came the questions and the counting—a new kind of reckoning amid the decay of civilized life. Miep Gies recounted that she and her husband Henk "and everyone else began waiting to see just who would be coming home to us. Shocking, unimaginable accounts circulated of the liberation of the German concentration camps. Pictures were printed in the first free newspaper; eyewitness information, too. Through the occupation we'd heard rumors of gassings, murder, brutality, poor living conditions in these camps, but none of us could have imagined such atrocities. The facts had far surpassed even our most pessimistic imaginings.... I needed to do everything I could to keep my optimism about our friends. It would have been unbearable to think otherwise."

Their friends included nine Jews in hiding in the secret annex above the offices where Gies had worked for Otto Frank's firm. Day after day, she asked returning Jews if they had seen any of the Frank family. In June, Otto Frank returned to The Netherlands from Auschwitz with the news that his wife had died there. He was unsure about what had happened to his two children, Margot and Anne. Months later, he got word from a nurse in Rotterdam that the daughters had not survived their imprisonment in Auschwitz and in Bergen-Belsen. The finality of all the deaths mixed into the tortured lives of those who survived. "I heard it said," Gies wrote in her book "that where the Jews had looked like everyone else before [the War], after what they had endured, those who returned looked different. But people hardly noticed because everyone had been through so much misery that no one had much interest in the suffering of others."[7] Despite the fact that Dutch Jewry lost nearly 75% of its population, the highest number of deaths in any Western

European country under occupation, despite the fact that Dutch Jewry had enjoyed an illustrious and secure existence in The Netherlands since the 16th century—certainly compared to Jewish communities in other European countries—and despite the fact that the Dutch Jews had lost everything—family, possessions, health—the few who came back were expected to make do with what they found or did not find of their former lives.

Frieda Menco was 15 when she returned from Auschwitz with her mother. They were the only survivors of their large family that had lived in The Netherlands for

6 Ibid, p. 227.

7 Ibid, p. 228.

over 300 years. "When we came back," she recalled, "we tried to tell people of our experiences. But nobody wanted to listen. The authorities considered us as a pain in the neck. A Jew who came back and wanted something." The survivors were told to forget and be quiet— to keep their nightmares and losses to themselves. A once thriving Jewish Dutch world of family, community, institutions, property and homes was gone. That was it. The Dutch constructed effective bureaucratic remedies to bury Jewish claims to emotional and full financial restitution. Many survivors retreated into silence as European countries began to rebuild, to cleanse themselves of some of the Nazis and to adjust to the development of the Iron Curtain.

Amidst rebuilding civilized life in the post-War world, Europeans and Americans constructed comforting wartime myths, especially myths about resistance. This is particularly true about the Dutch who sought to restore a viable nation after the trauma of occupation and the erosion of the pillar society. New terms of national unity, dependent on myths of resistance and victimization, were developed. In a seminal essay, Matthijs Kronemijer and Darren Teshima described this process. This new "identity was built upon the heroic stories of resistance in the Netherlands to the Nazi regime and the belief that Dutch society had stood by and protected its Jewish citizens. While individual acts of heroism and resistance certainly existed, the formation of a national myth focused on these acts and extending this heroism to describe the entire Dutch nation obfuscated the truth of the war experience."[8]

The world thinks that the Franks were emblematic of what happened to the Jews in the Netherlands. From Anne's story the international public has gained the impression that whole Jewish families could go into hiding together; that most could remain in one place for a few years; that numerous Christian friends or employees could sustain and succor them in hiding; and that the unfortunate hidden Jews were the ones betrayed by some unknown informer. And, the final impression: after the war, Dutch Jews would be welcomed back in the country in which they had lived.

In the Netherlands as in all other European countries, there were extremes of valor and decency along with villainy, greed, brutality and cowardice. In the large middle, there were the bystanders who lived with fear and indifference to the threatened minority. Within the Netherlands there were two extremes: on the one hand, mainly Communists and pious Protestants resistance fighters, including many protectors of Jews; and, on the other hand, collaborators who supported the deportation of Jews and the wholesale theft of Jewish property and possessions. At Yad Vashem in Israel and the U.S. Holocaust Memorial Museum in Washington, thousands upon thousands of Dutch are honored as Righteous Gentiles, including Miep Gies. Risking their lives, they had to resist not only the Germans but their fellow citizens as well. Dutch collaborators or Nazis—as well as rogues just desperate for money—hunted Jews down and turned them over to the authorities. In the official report about the Franks, the record simply states that someone was given the pitifully small amount of 60 guilders—seven guilders for each person he turned over

8 Kronemijer, Matthijs and Teshima, Darren, *Reflections on the Holocaust*, (Humanity in Action, Inc.), p.116.

in the Frank hideout.

The history of Otto Frank and his family, in fact, was unique in many ways. Most of the Dutch were too afraid of German terror and punishment to aid those in hiding; most Dutch people—Jew and Gentile alike—couldn't be sure that their neighbors could be trusted; most Dutch Jewish families were broken up as children were sent away by themselves into hiding; most of those in hiding had to move from place to place to escape detection; many Amsterdam Jewish families were too poor to pay for places to hide in the country of densely populated urban homes or in the flat terrain of villages and farms; most Jewish families had no assets of property and friendship among non-Jews to expend on survival, although a considerable number of Dutch protected Jews without initially asking for payment. And then after the war, most Dutch Jews came back to a society that was, in large part, indifferent—and at worst cruelly hostile—to what the Jews had suffered in the camps and what they had lost in regard to their family, home, work and communities. Again, Otto Frank was an exception. Miep Gies and her husband, who had protected and aided the Franks in hiding, received him warmly, brought him into their family for seven years and helped him to rebuild his life.

These exceptions never impinge on the myths. In the service of the redemptive legend of Anne Frank, there is a pattern of pilgrimage that starts and ends at 263 Princengracht in Amsterdam. People go to Anne Frank's house, beckoned by the *Diary* that has sold over 25 million copies in over 50 languages, to have contact with a consecrated space of suffering. They visit the house/museum, which is now supervised by an outstanding educational foundation. The hideout on the upper floors is a stifling, small space high up narrow stairs behind the typical central city's embellished facade of a narrow brick house. It is one of those typical Amsterdam houses set in rigid, repetitive formations between the canal in front and a garden behind. Canal, home and garden—all carefully planned to blend and separate the animated life on the street and canal with the quiet privacy on the inside. Big windows on the street bring light into the houses and exposure to the life of the city; transparent glass curtains unmistakably divide the public and private sphere of concern and responsibility.

The Dutch are somewhat appalled that the Anne Frank House is such an attraction for tourists—especially the Americans who pay homage to Holocaust remembrance. Nonetheless, this flood of attention, drawing 800,000 visitors a year to the House, is a convenience and distraction for the Dutch. It is also a lucrative source of Dutch tourism. Tourists don't dig deeper into the history. And the Dutch don't push the matter. Few of the visitors go beyond the house to explore the sad history of what happened to the rest of Dutch Jewry and to the Dutch themselves. Few visitors move on to other places, such as the Resistance Museum, that memorialize the history of opposition to the Germans and the fate of Dutch Jewry during the War. There are 800,000 visitors annually at the Anne Frank House, but only 19,000 visit the Hollandse Schouwburg, the former theatre where the Germans processed many Dutch Jews for deportation, although it too is now a museum and monument.

There is a clear irony relating to the book and the matter of return—not ours but Anne's. The 1950s public, including the Dutch, welcomed Anne Frank's miraculously preserved diary. But had she herself returned right after the war, few in The Netherlands would have wanted to learn about her suffering directly from her or through her writing. Testimony was not in style. After enduring the occupation, the impoverishment of the economy and public morale, the Dutch didn't want to hear about the camps, the theft of Jewish property by the Germans and the Dutch themselves, or have to account for the orderly disappearance of 110,000 Jews from 1942 to 1944.

There is, however, one place in Amsterdam, and maybe others as well, where the myth of Anne Frank does not flourish. This is in the social hall of the Liberal Jewish Synagogue. After attending a service in the sanctuary, one goes into an adjoining room to eat and socialize. On the central wall is a picture of Anne Frank age 12 — one that we have all seen numerous times. There is no written explanation on the wall—no attempt at identification, no attempt to make a monument or find meaning. Just a remembrance. The Franks lived near the original Liberal Jewish Synagogue before they went into hiding. They were members of the synagogue.

No one in the congregation needs any explanation for what happened to her. She is part of them, but also apart. In this place, there are no misconceptions, distractions or embellishments concerning the symbolic and real Anne. The same human tornado of persecution hit all of the families with the devastating loss of Jewish friends, progeny, community, family, confidence, habits, wealth, traditions and knowledge. The burden of living with that past is hard enough. Living in the somber shadows of Dutch tolerance, indifference, national victimization and the Anne Frank myth—the task is even harder.

Alone with Charlotte Salomon

Partisan Review, January 1, 2002

In 1994, the American historian Mary Lowenthal Felstiner published a biography about Charlotte Salomon, an artist who fled from Berlin to the South of France in 1939 and was deported four years later. At the age of 26 she was killed in Auschwitz. In between the flight from Germany and her forced departure to Poland, Salmon produced a corpus of over a thousand paintings. She placed over 730 of them, all gouaches paintings all of the same small size, in sequence to form a multi-dimensional oeuvre of unique pictorial expressions. Figures, landscapes, scenes, words and dialogue form autobiographical and family narratives and aesthetic, psychological and philosophical explorations. Felstiner's biography, resting on the testimony of these images, illuminated Salomon's family and social relationships within the debilitating political, social and emotional turmoil of Weimar Germany and the Nazi state.

In the concluding pages—a coda of sorts based upon the book's richest themes—Felstiner hoped that Salomon's work would finally gain proper recognition. "Life? or Theatre?" has still to reach other major museums of modern art," she wrote, "where all its inventions ought to place it with the avant-garde: it layered a drama over real events, trespassed single frames, infused colors with sounds, exposed a script on see-through overlays, mixed words into images. Its uniqueness has captivated some art historians, and future exhibits might feature not just the scenes but also those tragicomic overlays, or the taped-over studies, or the hidden life behind the characters, or the world of exile that weighted CS" arms down as she sketched, or the mystery of her method...."

Now when over 400 of Salomon's works are on display at the Jewish Museum in New York, on loan from the Joods Historisch Museum in Amsterdam, one would hope Salomon's moment has come. It did in London where the exhibition was shown at the Royal Academy and shepherded, explained and acclaimed by Norman Rosenthal, the Director. Unfortunately, judging from the initial reception by the New York press the response won't be as strong in the States. The question is why. What makes so many viewers undervalue, or slight her work in New York and Amsterdam as well? What keeps Salomon from a potentially huge public that is often drawn—in waves of acclaim or curiosity—to artistic expressions that are suggested or represented in Salomon's work?

The first reason may be expectations. Before actually seeing the paintings, critics and writers predispose viewers to look at Salomon's work in specific ways for certain purposes. The theologian Paul Tillich, in 1963 in one of the earliest publications about Salomon, praised her for being "universally human" and not dwelling on the horrors of the Holocaust. "But what makes this life a true symbol is something more than its universality. It is specifically the life of a very gifted and sensitive young woman, lived in one of the most terrible periods of European history, that speaks in the almost primitive simplicity of these pictures."[9]

When the works arrived in New York in December 2000, Michael Kimmelman, in the *New York Times*, sought to reverse the Tillich approach. "Put aside, as much as possible," he wrote, "the grim death that has boxed Salomon, like Anne Frank, into the eye-glazing, inviolate category of Holocaust artist, a disservice to her, distorting the real message of her work." Instead, he counseled that the viewer should regard her as a "gifted" artist who just worked "for the sake of it." According to Kimmelman, Salomon's artistic story is about love and art, idolized family and friends, worldly success and painful failures. The work he concluded, is a "coming-of-age story about a woman squeezing a whole life into one great gesture, and in the end her energy matters most, a civilizing energy. Becoming an artist really was a useless but indispensable act of spiritual preservation for her, and that is the work's ultimate lesson." (Unfortunately, the particular color reproduction chosen to accompany the review seems to justify that conclusion.) To the critic's eye, that futile and ambitious exercise was simply beyond her "abilities."[10]

Tillich and Kimmelman presented two very different evaluations of Salomon's work, but both dismissed her—and possibly did not seriously consider her—as an artist who is capable of challenging our understanding of art and allowing us see the world in different ways. Thus, these two approaches don't lead very far. And this may just be the beginning of the difficulties involved in appreciating Salomon's work. First and foremost, she doesn't fit into any familiar categories. The viewer is forced to approach Salomon's work on her self-imposed, rigorously defined, individualistic terms. She stood alone in her vision, broad scope and execution. Although she often made stylistic or figurative visual references to other artists, she foreclosed every avenue of artistic similarity by her independence and original artistic expression.

Even describing the work, as opposed to explaining it, presents initial difficulties. In fact, exactly what does Salomon's "Life? or Theatre?" consist of? It is a series of over 700 striking images, set in precise order, frequently informed by descriptive explanatory text that was placed within the image itself or on an overlay of tracing paper. The individual gouaches form a narrative of events as well as intellectual and psychological reflections that create an autobiographical/fictional account of Charlotte Salomon's life. It is an elusive story, presented to inform both through

9 *Charlotte: A Diary in Pictures* by Charlotte Salomon, Introduction.

10 *New York Times*, December 29, 2000, pp. 39, 41.

truths and distortions, told from multiple perspectives of actions and thoughts of characters that Salomon created to personify her history and feelings. It is a deeply complex work that needs to be approached on the different levels of the narrative itself, the intellectual ruminations and the emotional explorations—all expressed through the cumulative succession of artistic images.

Salomon didn't join, and posthumously doesn't belong, to any school or category. She had no artistic mentors or confreres—no group of talented friends or enemies—whom history honors or finds interesting. In her work, one can discern vague signs of the future art of the 1960s through the 1990s—the monomaniacal word-art of Jenny Holtzer, the repetitious imagery of Andy Warhol or Gilbert and George; or the fixation on self in the manipulated identities of Cindy Sherman. Salomon's experimentation, however, never exceeded the boundaries of 8x10 gouache paintings. And into a continuous, repetitive and conventional format she placed the unconventional substance of her work. Salomon's work, although held together through a powerful narrative thread, doesn't respond to any historical theme or embellish any established mythologies. And finally, her work doesn't carry the slightest tinge of commercial value. The gouache paintings had little monetary value when she was alive and almost none since her death. A handful may be available on the art market. Therefore, they don't entice the collector, whether it be a museum or individual, and entrance the public with fairy tales of unforeseen fame and wealth.

"Salomon doesn't belong to any place or nation—not to Berlin, the city where she grew up, but the city that threw her out; not to the South of France where she created her work, but from which she was removed and sent off to Poland; and not to The Netherlands, where her work "Life? *or Theatre?*" eventually found a permanent home, but a city that she had never seen."

Salomon doesn't belong to any place or nation—not to Berlin, the city where she grew up, but the city that threw her out; not to the South of France where she created her work, but from which she was removed and sent off to Poland; and not to The Netherlands, where her work "Life? or Theatre?" eventually found a permanent home, but a city that she had never seen. The Dutch connection was due to her father Alfred Solomon, a distinguished doctor and her stepmother, Paula Salomon-Lindberg, who was a renowned operatic singer. After Charlotte left Berlin for France in 1939, her father and stepmother fled to Amsterdam. They hid after the German invasion in 1940, were captured and sent to the Westerbork camp for rerouting to the East. They escaped, hid once again, and, after the war, gratefully lived out their lives in Amsterdam. Felstiner wrote that once when Charlotte's step mother returned to Berlin for an exhibition of Charlotte's work, she covered her eyes to avoid viewing parts of the city which had shattered her family and destroyed her career.

According to a friend, when asked in her declining years, as she became increasingly reconnected to Germany, if she would prefer to speak German rather than Dutch, Paula emphatically replied: "Aber Ich spreche doch immer Hollandisch."

But Charlotte Salomon herself had no connection or affinity with the Dutch. Thus she is not now, nor will she ever be an icon of Dutch art. And unlike Anne Frank, Salomon will never be a Dutch icon of Dutch victimization. Ironically and unexpectedly, recognition came to both families through their daughters, although Salomon and Frank's reputations are hardly to be compared. The parallel histories between Charlotte and Anne Frank are clear: both were German Jews who fled to another country; both died young; both families experienced temporary refuge in Amsterdam and subsequent imprisonment in Westerbork; both young women had a parent or parents who survived the war, remained in Amsterdam and became part of the shattered Dutch Jewish community that barely survived the Holocaust. Both the Salomons and Franks knew little of their daughters' talents and nothing until after the War of their works that miraculously survived. Both families sought to excise and edit embarrassing aspects of their daughters' creations.

All of these factors relate to the background and aura surrounding Salomon's work. But there are other complicating limitations in the direct confrontation with Salomon's art that also discourage interest. When one finally confronts the art on the walls of a museum, in New York or Amsterdam, one sees only a sampling or selection—all the same sized, neatly framed images—drawn from "Life? or Theatre?" (The catalogue provides the only way to access the complete works.) And what do they show? What do they require? They demand time, concentration and a new way of looking and thinking about art. For by design and creative instinct, Salomon moved back and forth between reality and fantasy, history and reinvention, memories and reenactments, secrets and lies, humor and pathos, sardonic spoofing and profound thought, unfulfilled desires and needs, hurts, failures, hopes and loves—all formulated through her particular artistic expression.

The facts of her actual history illuminate Salomon's work only up to a point as she combined narrative, emotion, recollections, thought and musical references in imagery and text. She evoked the searing history of a tragic family, personal isolation and uncertainties about her strengths and stability and the tortured times of Jewish life in Europe from the First to the Second World Wars. A family suffering from emotional illness and suicides. A child desperately wanting but lacking affection—unsure of herself, jealous of others, confused and unhappy. An adolescent looking for recognition, inspiration, direction, spiritual and physical love. A European woman armed with enlightened intellectual and cultural tools of art, philosophy, music, psychoanalytic thought and religion. A woman capturing and then rearranging the lives and interactions of her family and friends (especially the triangular relationships involving herself, her mentor Alfred Wolfsohn and her step-mother Paula Salomon-Lindberg), manipulating them back and forth between actual personalities and theatrical characters. A Jewish woman, frightened and furious over vicious persecution which closed in on her life and that of her family.

Salomon talked through images and painted through words. On sheet upon sheet of notebook sized paper, she staged her history and fantasies, setting images upon musical references. She moved through experiences, family stories and feelings in depicting a carefully constructed agglomeration of figures and interior and exterior landscapes— sometimes carefully separated, but often magically spilling over into each other. She painted thousands of memories and imaginings, internal and external conversations and feelings. Sometimes only one image on a page; sometimes a vertiginous multiplicity. Sometimes she imposed thoughts from text outside the picture; sometimes words flowed directly out of the brains or mouths of her characters. Sometimes she used tones of detachment and distance; at other times, the fiery intensity of the deepest emotions.

Salomon did all of this frenzied work, driven by the force of creativity and controlled by discipline, skill and mastery of multiple artistic forms. The need to know, understand, recollect, confront, express, hope and create—all of this she accomplished with creative self-restraint. She was absorbed in her history and desire to escape madness, chaos and futility—but not possessed by self-absorption. She refused to stay the eternal child or the beleaguered adolescent. She moved on to adulthood through personal, social and professional encounters—real and imagined—that were daring, painful, explicit, probing and honest.

Ultimately, no stylistic simplicity or simplistic explanations describes Salomon's work. Norman Rosenthal's introduction to the exhibition catalogue provides the most enlightened, succinct summation about the work. It exists, he wrote, on three levels: the first is that of "individual experience;" the second reveals what Rosenthal calls "an entire cultural milieu;" and the third, "the plan of the imagination."[11] What these levels reveal will differ from viewer to viewer. But they have the unique potential to expand and uplift a viewer's understanding of art and life. As European anti-Semitism spewed forth in 1939, the year that Salomon fled to France, a non-Jewish friend of the Romanian writer Mihail Sebastian remarked to him: "J'aime les Juifs. Je les aimes passionement. Ce n'est pas parce qu'ils sont malheureux. Non. Je les aime parce qui'ils eloignent l'horizon.")[12] Salomon extended her horizon and ours—what more can a great artist do?

---

11 *Charlotte Salomon, Life? or Theatre*, Introduction.

12 Sebastian, Mihail, *Journal: 1935-1944*, p. 209.

Reflections on Humanity in Action

2013

Almost 16 years ago, a former French Resistance fighter, a Jew and immigrant in America, posed a perplexing question when we met for the first time for a serious conversation: how do we educate young people about the need to resist oppressive, authoritarian forces? The query came out of the blue to me but clearly not to this survivor, successful businessman, father of four children and philanthropist. He wanted an answer right away. I was hardly prepared for the challenge. I had read about European resistance movements, especially in Scandinavia, but was hardly knowledgeable.

Seemingly out of nowhere I put forth an idea: why not identify a small group of smart, socially conscious university students in Denmark and the United States, put them together in Copenhagen for several weeks of inquiry into Danish history during World War II and let them probe the deeper explanations for the unique national rescue of the Danish Jewish population. Somewhat desperate to do something, he said he liked the idea. Could I put such a program together? I said yes. Could he find the financial resources to develop a program? He said yes.

A year later, we started the Danish-American Dialogue on Human Rights in Copenhagen with 10 American and 10 Danish university students. It was a project of Thanks to Scandinavia, an American organization dedicated to promoting knowledge of Scandinavian resistance during the World War II and providing scholarships to Scandinavian students for study in the US. The time was right: European social welfare states were thriving; the Cold War was over; Human Rights provided the ideology of international aspiration for idealistic youth; the Holocaust and World War II remained vital concerns, subject to historical studies, education and processes of restitution. Europe, except for the Balkans, appeared on the surface to be free of pernicious national, religious, racial and ethnic tensions.

In 1995 we put together a small advisory group to select the American Fellows and sent out notice of the program to hundreds of American four-year academic institutions seeking outstanding applicants. We depended upon a remarkable committee of Danish journalists and historians, headed by Herbert Pundik, the editor-in-chief of the newspaper "Politiken," to select Danish Fellows and to identify a broad range of speakers of the highest quality. The small organizational staffs in Denmark and the United States were tasked with informing the Fellows about the history of World War II, individual and group behavior, values and the complexities of Danish political, religious, cultural, economic and international issues. For the American students, the program began at the United States Holocaust Memorial Museum working closely with its educational and research staff.

Our aim was not to engage in a romantic whitewash, simply extolling the heroism of the Danes but investigate the unique historic circumstances—as well as choices and values—of that society. The Fellows were to work hard in a cooperative, international exploration of Denmark's immediate past and present and, in the final week, team with an international partner to write and publish cutting edge journalist report. At the end of two years the program was a success from the perspectives of the 40 American and Danish students and project staffs. Thanks to Scandinavia, however, decided to focus on other educational areas.

The idea of the fellowship, however, had taken root with the Fellows and funders. With amazing speed, the two-year experiment was transformed into Humanity in Action, a US based non-for-profit educational organization. It established a board of directors in the United States, maintained its Danish supporters and sought to expand its reach beyond Denmark. Guided by the Danish advisory board, The Netherlands was designated as the second country to incorporate in the European educational effort. Ed van Thijn, a political leaders and former Mayor of Amsterdam, established a Dutch board. In June 1999, Humanity in Action organized two five-week summer programs for a group of 40 university students from Denmark, The Netherlands and the United States that focused on diversity and human rights issues in the two European countries.

The educational objectives were ambitious, experimental and idealistic: engage and mentor outstanding Fellows through exposure to an eclectic set of scholars, writers, government officials and activists; provide rigorous programs; encourage action through civic engagement with particular focus on responsibility towards ones own country; require Fellows to create action projects after the summer programs; enter the broad field of human rights programs; maintain focus on genocide, the Holocaust and World War II for their absolute historical importance and significance for contemporary minority and human rights issues; and expand summer programs to include more European countries; and create a vibrant network of alumni, dedicated to the organization's political and moral issues, to benefit the Fellows as they pursued their professional careers and further the aims of the foundation. Clearly, the future of the Fellows would be intertwined with ours. We, however, did not know exactly what that would mean.

We shaped rigorous programs that were international, interdisciplinary and intergenerational. We entered the field of university oriented educational programs without the institutional support or financial backing of a major foundation, academic institution or non-for-profit. We were on our own taking risks, making adjustments when required and constantly looking for new programmatic opportunities to enrich the Fellows. We were also perpetually in fund-raising mode that required constantly explaining and justifying the complex educational mission and program.

Embedded in the tendency towards flexibility and opportunistic expansion, there were fundamental ideas and methods that grounded our approach. We engaged college and university students on the assumption that they were sufficiently well educated and inquisitive to explore the nature of conflict, including the behavior of perpetrators, resisters and bystanders. We expected that the Fellows would be mature enough to handle the social, intellectual and psychological pressures of intense and constant dialogue in an international group and setting. We sought Fellows from diverse backgrounds—ethnic, religious, racial and economic—pursuing a broad range of professional careers. We would pay the costs of all Fellows to insure the inclusion of those who might lack adequate financial resources. We would require post-summer program action projects to insure that the Fellows reached out to a broader public beyond the narrow contours of the small summer cohort.

We insisted upon collaborative learning in connecting past to present as an effective way to gain knowledge, facilitate understanding and build sustained connections and trust for future action to benefit the Fellows, Humanity in Action, civic society and the Trans-Atlantic relationships. We were determined to maintain a program dedicated to minority and diversity issues but not just for minorities or any particular minority. Although the historic focus central to the program was on the Holocaust, we would not seek or accept designation as a Jewish organization. We would organize programs only in democratic societies in the Europe and North America. We would explore minority issues in the context of identity, attitudes and histories in the Humanity in Action designated- countries—but not on a global scale. We expected that the particular national focus would enable Fellows to think more broadly and comparatively about their own domestic minority issues. We would rely on the national boards and staffs to form the highest quality programs about history, culture and contemporary minority issues in their own countries.

“We were determined to maintain a program dedicated to minority and diversity issues but not just for minorities or any particular minority.

Over the years we have been challenged—and challenged ourselves—to revaluate and justify the subject matter, concepts and broad goals by board members, staff, donors, potential donors, government officials and others. Were we targeting the most valuable and strategically important age group? Why focus on World War II and Holocaust instead of colonial histories, the Balkans, Darfur, and America's racial history as the base for exploring minority issues? What impact could a comparatively small program have on public issues of prejudice, discrimination, divided societies and extremists devoted to violent, destabilizing practices and goals? What is the relationship between study and action? What constitutes an effective alumni network? And finally, how would we measure success?

We have addressed these questions as we have expanded from the initial base of summer programs in Denmark and The Netherlands. At first, we tested enlargement by establishing a program in Germany engaging a total of 60 Fellows in the three summer programs. Building upon that successful integration in 2006 we boldly established programs in France and Poland. We also established a US program based in New York that focused on black/white and immigration issues, consistent with exploring diversity issues. After the 2008 recession, however, we were unable to sustain funding for the US based program. Nonetheless, we have continued to increase the number of participants in five national European programs to total over 100 each year, by including Fellows from Bosnia, the Ukraine and Turkey.

The Programs

In the dynamic process of self-critical inquiry by the boards and staff we have sought to find cogent answers that transcend mission statements and organizational messaging. The programs are under constant review and the educational methods are ever subject to improvement. In fact, revisiting the basic educational subjects and methods is essential to the organization's ambitious and dynamic means of exploring critical historical and contemporary issues.

The answers to some of the questions are built upon an integrated base of programmatic concepts and methodology. The first major aspect for review concerns the university population. The consensus is that university students are the most promising and important ones to engage as many of them are on the edge of transformative thought and action. Walter Laqueur in an article about Europe in the 1920s, quoted Martin Buber on the potential of youth in their 20s and 30s. "Youth," Buber wrote, "is the eternal chance that mankind possesses." Laqueur expanded on the theme: "Older generations generally focus on the difficulties, dangers, and risks of political change. But young people have always had the passion, idealism and enthusiasm to struggle for political change." The optimism, however, was well tempered for Laqueur who apprehensively cited the young age of the Italian and German fascists and many of the Russian Communist revolutionaries. Buber was even more pessimistic about the course of eternal hope and opportunity of younger generations. The reality of youth is often different. "What a pity," he wrote, "this chance is usually wasted."[13]

At the heart of Humanity in Action is the desire and responsibility not to waste the potential of youth—to engage the passion, idealism, entrepreneurial dynamism and facility with communications that are boldly manifested in younger people today. No previous generation of young people has ever participated in, led and significantly profited from a major technological and communications breakthrough. Of equal importance is the fact that younger generations in Europe and America have grown up in societies that recognize the importance of human rights, including those of

13 Laquer, Walter, *New Republic*, August 2, 2013, p. 16.

minorities, and distribute widespread benefits to all their citizens. While some young people still gravitate to extremists, racist and xenophobic parties, the greater number profit from diversity. They often lead societies towards more liberal, tolerant attitudes and policies in regard to gender, ethnicity and race. Significant numbers are globally well traveled in pursuit of service, development and educative projects. Surprisingly, they have done so much that by the time some of them join the Humanity in Action programs, they feel they have exhausted their idealism and sense of purpose by too many disappointing, unproductive engagements abroad and at home.

The second major area for reconsideration has been the focus on World War II and the Holocaust. From year to year Fellows and board members question the organization's commitment to the primacy and relevance of the Holocaust for the Humanity in Action European summer programs. (The single programmatic departure from this historical reference was American program that lasted three years.) In part, this discussion emanates from Holocaust fatigue, especially in European countries. This attitude, sometimes expressed outwardly but often hidden in unspoken undercurrents of thought, assumes that there has been sufficient public and educational focus on the Holocaust and the victimization of Jewish populations. The debts of guilt, it is maintained, have been paid off through ample restitution and public expressions of remembrance and memorialization.

While taking these perspectives into account, the Humanity in Action boards have continually reaffirmed the centrality of World War II and Holocaust to the organization's mission. It is precisely by trying to understand that cataclysmic event, ever subject to new analyses, that the boards have reinforced their commitment to an integrated set of educational and moral responsibilities to the past and present. The programs adhere to the view of historian Irving Howe: "the Holocaust remains a problem that can be neither resolved nor abandoned."[14]

Western societies still live with the deep shadows of perpetrators, collaborators, bystanders and resisters—assigning culpability, honoring defiance and understanding the actions in between. Thus, the ongoing challenge to gain knowledge of the causes and consequences of the German inspired political and military upheaval that enabled the country to conquer, exploit and crush European nations. As those in the West sought to recover from genocide and ethnic cleansing, they constructed blueprints for recovery based upon the recognition of moral degradation and the frightening capacity to maim and destroy cultures and populations. The postwar Western European and American societies, however, were not built just on fears of repeating the past. They chose an architecture of renewal built with democratic procedures, social welfare states, rule of law and human rights—rights that specifically provide protection for minorities from the pernicious potential of state power and lawlessness.

An examination of the history of World War II and Holocaust allows the Fellows to confront critical questions about human behavior, the legacies of the recent past

14 Blatter, Janet and Milton, Sybil, *Art of the Holocaust*, p. 11.

and our contemporary challenges. It provides a moral and intellectual compass to engage in the complex present day minority issues that inform and affect the cohesiveness and degrees of equity in our democracies. It opens up awareness of what Profs. Robert Futrell and Pete Simi call the "hidden spaces of hate" which are still prevalent in our European and American societies. Those spaces, specifically part of extremist political movement in the US and Europe, provide the breeding grounds for attacks based on race, ethnicity and gender.

We make concerted efforts to provide clarity for Fellows about the topics we include and methods that we use. Despite the recognized focus on World War II and Holocaust, many Fellows bring priorities based upon different national and individual ways of judging human rights and minority issues. Despite the fact that summer Fellows enter the program acknowledging its basic structure and mission, many struggle during the program itself to accept Humanity in Action's conceptual and nationally based boundaries. Diversity issues that reverberate in all the Humanity in Action countries are intellectually and emotionally powerful for Fellows. By focusing on minority issues within one country, the Fellows automatically confront the wounds of class, race, religious and gender superiority and discrimination and power dynamics that prevail in a specific country but inevitably, they reflect back to their own countries.

Humanity in Action seeks to find the pedagogical balance between a Fellow's desire to reach out to others through exposure to different backgrounds and beliefs with the compelling need to find acceptance and validation based upon ones own individual and group identity. At best this tension provides the personal and collective ground for building respect, confidence and long-term trust that cross borders. The Fellows benefit from gaining greater knowledge about another country as well as insights about their own native country. Fellows learn both from expert speakers but most significantly from continual peer-to-peer discussions that blend the native knowledge of the Fellows from the host country with perspectives of Fellows from abroad.

The summer program is explicitly designed to establish a mechanism and prototype for understanding and overcoming some of the deeply enduring tensions related to personal and group differences, including a tendency to competitive victimization. The educational method meets the subject matter of diversity and minorities head on. We work to make difficult intellectual and emotional discussions honest, frank and constructive—to emphasize the advantages and recognize the difficulties cited in *Education's End: Why our Colleges and Universities have given up on the Meaning of Life* by Prof. Anthony Kronman:

> When individuals exchange views as individuals, they converse. Their exchange is characterized by the flexibility that is the hallmark of every real conversation. This is true even if their views are different or antagonistic. By contrast, when two meet as representatives, they speak not on behalf of themselves but of the groups to which they belong. It is to the group,

> not to their interlocutor or to the conversation in which they are engaged, that their loyalty is owed....The individuals exchanging views cease to be individuals, and their exchange ceases to be a conversation. Its personal significance for them declines and its political importance as a negotiation increases.[15]

The challenges inherent in the Humanity in Action educational method—intense personal and collective conversations about diversity in a diverse group—are inextricably connected to the complex focus of the programs: understanding the basic needs and benefits of identifying with a nation, religion, race, class, gender and ethnic group while resisting the proclivity for one group to dominate, degrade and even attempt to destroy another. The complex tensions are ones that Harvard Professor Edward O. Wilson wrote about in *The Social Conquest of the World*. Seeking to understand the roots of human and animal evolution through group selection, he emphasized the inherent forces of evolution and the contradictory needs and proclivities of human nature and societies—aspects that drive "a great deal of what is most typical—and perplexing—about human nature." Wilson insisted "that people feel compelled to belong to groups and, having joined, consider them superior to competing groups." And yet being part of a group doesn't resolve contradictory needs that drive human behavior:

> Multilevel selection (group and individual selection combined) also explains the conflicted nature of motivations. Every normal person feels the pull of conscience, of heroism against cowardice, of truth against deception, of commitment against withdrawal. It is our fate to be tormented with large and small dilemmas as we daily wind our way through the risky, fractious world that gave us birth.[16]

Humanity in Action addresses some of those large human dilemmas though its focus on emerging leaders, the relationships among minority and majority populations, resistance, collaborative learning, history and contemporary events. It is a constant challenge as the boundaries of our knowledge of history, education and human behavior expand and the political, social and cultural circumstances of our lives change. We must revisit our presumptions and renew our efforts to understand issues that preclude resolution—tensions involving universal human rights, rule of law, the proclivity to violence and the authority of the nation or state.

Each Humanity in Action program presents a unique experiment in collective learning—mixing multiple national, interntional, individual and groups perspectives—through the interaction of the Fellows, staff, boards and speakers. Every year presents new challenges of evaluation for the programs, especially now when Europe's post-war blueprint for binding unification and cooperation is under

15 Kronman, Anthony, *Education's End: Why our Colleges and Universities have given up on the Meaning of Life*, p. 150.

16 Wilson, Edward O. *The Social Conquest of the World*, p.290.

stress. Now we need to ask if European populations are neglecting the toxic past of national, religious and ethnic tensions of the 20th Century. Are the post-war years in fact anomalous due to the creation of homogeneous Western European welfare states that honored human rights, the protection of minorities and the imperative of peaceful solutions to conflicts? Is decisive collective action among disparate European countries sustainable?

Fourteen years after founding Humanity in Action, its pedagogy puts its philosophy into practice. The organization remains anchored in rigorous educational explorations about diversity and promoting resistance to injustice in Europe, America and other parts of the world. Based in seven countries, its trans-Atlantic reach now goes significantly beyond the boarders of Humanity in Action countries through the active work and interests of its Senior Fellows. Large number of the 1,200 Senior Fellows are converting collaborative learning and trust—incorporating historic examples such as the collective rescue of Danish Jews based on shared national values—into productive action on an individual and group basis. In response to the aspirations and desire for continuing education of the Senior Fellows, we have generated an array of substantive programs including annual conferences, study trips, and professional fellowships; authored Reflections on the Holocaust, a book of essays by Senior Fellows and speakers; and commissioned "Just People," a documentary film about conflict and resistance.

To reach beyond the immediate Humanity in Action community, the Fellows have generated hundreds of action plans on an individual and group basis that connect them across different annual summer programs and countries. Extensive evidence of their entrepreneurial spirit and professional advancement is one of the organization's greatest assets. The continuing interaction of the Fellows with each other, through and beyond the organization, is an important contribution to the emerging power of social networks. Through education and action that confirms the power of human rights, the commitment of the organization—its Senior Fellows, board members and staffs in 7 countries—reaffirms the precious promise of youth. It is a promise that could not have been revealed so boldly without the guidance and financial support of many visionary philanthropists, in the United States and Europe. It is their faith in the importance of youth and change that has enabled Humanity in Action to prosper and look confidently with younger generations into the future.

The Presence of the Past: Confronting the Nazi State and Jim Crow

2011

Well into the second decade of the 21st Century, both the United States and Germany struggle with the consequences of previous state sponsored racist beliefs and behaviors. Neither the end of the Nazi state in 1945 nor the elimination of Jim Crow laws in the 1960s and 1970s has fully eradicated the lethal circuits of discrimination and violence.

A report, issued in January 2012 by a panel of experts appointed by the Bundestag, states that one out of five Germans holds anti-Semitic views, encouraged by extreme right wing organizations and internet sites.[17] Mein Kampf is still barred from publication in Germany for fear that it will find popular support. Germans do not use the word "race" in any discourse and avoid the word "racism" in normal and even scholarly discussions despite the fact that Germany now experiences serious religious, cultural and ethnic tensions among its increasingly diverse population.

In the US, vitriolic partisan discussions are indisputably infused with racial tensions through code words and viral animosity towards the first black President. Questioning the legality of the Obama Presidency can only be attributed to an irrational belief that a black man should not be President and does not deserve the respect and legitimacy of the office.

Indisputably a host of serious economic, cultural, religious and ethnic issues, especially those aimed at Hispanics and Muslims, continue to agitate large parts of the American public and impact elections. But there is little question that the hot wires of racism have intensified the movement of the Republican Party towards deeply conservative, angry and even radical positions vis-à-vis the centrist inclinations of the vast majority of Americans.

In both the United States and Germany these attitudes embody the residue of deep-rooted histories of racism and discrimination. Examining and juxtaposing the racist policies of the segregated Jim Crow South and the Third Reich is one way to illuminate the current political landscapes that trouble both societies. At first glance, comparing might seem excessive and distorted in regard both to the intentions of

17 http://www.bbc.co.uk/news/world-europe-16678772

the oppressors and the suffering and losses of the victims. The differences between the two are sharp and stark. Over at least eight decades after the Civil War, the South oppressed its black population while Germany expelled and then annihilated its Jewish population as well as millions under Nazi occupation. Over the span of just one decade, anti-Semitism evolved from zealous denunciations, propaganda and prejudice to systematic mass murder through starvation, executions and extermination camps. The South, however, depended on generations of racist customs and learned behaviors—preceded by centuries of slavery—that were based in its legal systems and grounded in violence.

Germany was thoroughly defeated by military conquest and occupation. Jim Crow bowed to federal, state and local legislation, conforming to decisions of the Supreme Court, the federal judiciary and national legislation backed by military force of the federal government. The German Jewish population was eviscerated. The slow, tangled retreat from Jim Crow—both peaceful and violent—took place in America's heterogeneous society through heroic civil resistance, political and legal confrontations.

Despite these profound differences, it is instructive to bring together—into one focus—two distinct but complementary racist systems that reigned on two Western continents for 14 tumultuous years. On one side of the Atlantic, segregation bound the black population in abject legal, economic, political, social and cultural subjugation; on the other side, anti-Jewish laws and policies provided a raison d'être of the resurgent German people and militant state. Sympathetic in belief and practice throughout the 1930s, the two systems demonized racial groups (Jews as well as Gypsies in Europe and Native Americans in the US), extolled the eugenics movement, lionized male superiority and military culture, sanctified the domestication and political passivity of white and Aryan women and employed terror and violence to crush resistance to the systems.

The bonds of racist affinity broke when Germany declared war on America in December 1941, followed by the mobilization of American manpower, highly dependent upon Southern men, and the democratic crusade against the Fascists. Four years later, the Allies destroyed and demonized the German racial state and its hold over the countries it had conquered. But the triumphant international crusade for democracy and freedom stopped at Southern borders where Jim Crow continued to thrive. Nor did the crusade significantly diminish racial discrimination in the rest of the US. It took another two decades for the civil rights campaign to discredit nationwide prejudice and undermine and overpower the South's racial system—a second emancipation based upon the principles of the Declaration of Independence and American Constitution.

The racist state came first in the American South. The victory of the Union forces in1865 led to the official federally inspired eradication of slavery. By the turn of the century, however, the oppression of blacks had mutated into legally mandated segregation of whites and blacks and the full development of the Jim Crow state. It enabled Southern whites simultaneously to subjugate blacks, recover from wartime defeat and Reconstruction, and reconcile with the North. Segregation, a continuing investment in the repression of blacks, was based upon exclusion, impotence and the devaluation of black life. The noxious system of Jim Crow was inextricably embedded in the recesses of political, legal, economic, social, religious and cultural life in the South, implicating everyone who lived in the region. Without the complicity of almost the entire white South—through every level of the society—the system could not have survived decade after decade.

No longer an expansionist force based on slavery, in the post-Civil War years the rest of the country and the federal government permitted the South to sustain itself as a regional racist atrocity. While Jim Crow's convoluted legal permutations were confined to the South, prejudice against blacks was endemic beyond its borders to the north and west. Regions outside the South supported the new racial system though political compromise to stabilize the federal government and the two party system. Equally important were nationally shared habits of discrimination against blacks, pervasive prejudice, underpinnings of violence and willful ignorance about the punishing depths of Jim Crow.

Ironically, national acquiescence enabled Jim Crow to defy and betray America's hallowed basic founding creed of equality and liberty for its citizens—a creed that justified American expansion and power century after century. Throughout the late nineteenth century and first three decades of the twentieth, the American South was the single most significant area in Western Europe and North America to challenge the international trend towards liberal societies based on Enlightenment ideals of equal rights and democratic practices irrespective of race or ethnicity. Despite the flow of liberalism, the South found significant support for its racist beliefs from influential social scientists, scientists and authors on both side of the Atlantic. They advocated the pseudo-scientific dogmas of the eugenics movement that promoted racial hierarchies, separation and purification.

Preying upon popular fears, politicians frequently thrust the ideas of racial categorization, especially with long-developed anti-Semitic strains, into political platforms and electoral campaigns. American ideologues of racial categorization achieved major victories in the 1920s, when they prevailed upon the Congress to reduce drastically the number of Slavic, Italian, and Jewish immigrants. (Chinese and Japanese immigrants had been barred from entry since the late nineteenth century.)

No American legislative victories, however, compared to the stunning rise in 1933 of the fascist German state and racist leader, popularly elected and accepted by established German leaders. While prejudice and discrimination against many ethnic and religious groups was rampant in America and some European countries, only the American South and Germany—and ultimately countries under German occupation—constructed racial states that inflicted terror and deadly damage on their enemies.

From the perspective of doctrinaire Southern racists, Hitler's victories affirmed the validity and viability of a violence-based system of segregation and subordination.

On his part, Hitler both taunted America's so-called democracy and seized upon the American South as a positive reference for his racist regime. He was right. There were striking similarities between the two societies in the 1930s, especially in regard to the roles of men and women. Both idealized and enforced male dominance, military prowess and violence against their enemies: in the Third Reich, Aryan warriors as pagan gods and, in the South, white males as Confederate heroes as part of the "honor" culture. Both racist systems depended upon the critical docility, acquiescence and political impotence of women: designated as saints of the home, domestic heroes to husbands, children, society and the state. Germany and the South extolled the sexual purity of white—and in the German sphere—white Aryan women. Both targeted and exaggerated the threat of predatory men—blacks in the South and Jews in Germany—to justify intimidation and violence against the racial enemies.

Governments in the South and Germany depended on the service of women to the racial states. Their support fueled and reinforced fears and hatreds. Although allowed to vote, white women had no place in active political life and elective office. Nonetheless, they did not need political power to benefit in non-political ways from their idealized status in service to the racial state. (It is important to note, however, that many white women in the South led campaigns to oppose lynching.) Cate Haste's description of the position of women in Nazi Germany is equally applicable to women in the South. Women gained from "the esteem they could expect in their prescribed role as wives and mothers—the bearers of children to build the future Reich, the carriers of Nazi German culture into the next generation, and the source of eternally patient suffering and enduring love."[18] In the national theatre of Nazi propaganda, festive ceremonies were held to reward women for bearing children for the Third Reich.

In both societies physical intimidation, imprisonment and violent death were potent weapons to build and sustain the racial states. While women rarely engaged in physical brutality, they could hardly ignore the savage underpinning of the racial state that enabled them—no matter what their social and economic standing—to be superior to blacks in the South and Jews in Germany. A toxic mixture of dread and anxiety fueled the acclaimed divisions between superior and inferior groups in both societies. From generation to generation, based on intense memories of the Civil War and Reconstruction, Southerners were terrified of black rebellion and revenge – revenge that they often feared would take the form of rape. They feared the loss of authority, privilege and cheap labor, particularly in parts of the lower South where blacks outnumbered whites. In Germany hatred and fear were founded on popular projections, writ into law after 1933, of a world wide Jewish conspiracy and pollution of the Aryan race. Jews were considered vermin, parasites on a society trying to perfect itself into a pure Aryan state with a superior type of human being.

Beyond the similarities, the dynamics of segregation and separation also reveal crucial differences in the political, military, economic and social histories of the two

18 Haste, Cate, *Nazi Women*, p. 9.

racial states. One was expansive, the other static. To the German fascist mind in the 1930s, racial threats justified war, the expropriation of Jewish wealth on a massive scale and genocide. For the Southern mind, the racial society reinforced containment and the post-Reconstruction status quo. Categorizing and separating races was essential in both societies but the demonized races were not identical. In Germany, Jews were identified as dangerous, manipulative aliens, while blacks, regarded as inferior, were hardly a threat to the Third Reich. In the South, Jews were included as part of the entitled white society. although they faced some discrimination and prejudice. In Germany, racist beliefs were personified and internalized through a charismatic leader, penetrating all aspects of private and public life. The South, with generations of inherited racial beliefs taught within the families and schools, had no such need of an iconic, quasi-religious figure or even a small coterie of leaders to sustain segregation. It was simply assumed to be a permanent part of the natural God-ordained order of things. Anti-Jewish laws were applicable in all parts of Germany; in America, the draconian Jim Crow system prevailed only in the South, while other parts of America resorted to less severe forms of discrimination.

In Germany, law upon law divided Jews from other Germans, stripping away citizenship, wealth, educational opportunities, professional positions and social associations. Proximity to Jews was abhorred. Jewish men were depicted as lecherous and infected. Marriage and all sexual and personal relationships between Aryans and Jews were strictly forbidden. German women under 35 years of age could not work in Jewish homes. Nazi ideology foreclosed all contact with Jews except to inflict harm and plunder Jewish wealth. National Socialism pursued the purification of the Aryan race by assaulting and annihilating its own German Jewish population and, later, Jews in occupied countries. Ultimately, the urge to expel and exterminate Jews was economically self-defeating for the Nazis, as they could not bring themselves to benefit, on a broad scale, from contact with Jews and the exploitation of Jewish labor.

Cultural, political and economic needs, developed and reinforced over centuries in the South, dictated radically different forms of racial separation from those in Germany. The white South was heavily dependent on a large supply of black agricultural, industrial and domestic labor and, to a significant extent, on practices that were, in the words of historian Douglas Blackmon, only "slavery by another name." There was nothing to steal from blacks except their labor and the largely theoretical possibility they might develop equity and assets of their own. Opportunities to own property, establish businesses, participate in government and enjoy upward mobility were for whites only. They were the sole owners and exploiters of the vast, rich resources of the American continent and its growing population. The system of exploitation was most potent in the South, but de facto economic and social discrimination practiced throughout the country severely restricted black social mobility.

The intricate web of exclusion and segregation, enforced by punitive laws and social mores, penetrated all levels of Southern life: separate schools, separate facilities, separate claims of law. But the separation had a peculiar aspect: the need for black labor created a servant class of black men, women and children who formed an integral part of white households. Interaction was close. Intimacy was the result. Familiar affection between blacks and whites frequently developed. White women and children often developed deep emotional bonds and dependency on blacks but always within the context of white superiority and the inescapable mechanisms that imposed obedience and humiliation on blacks. While racist ideology, drawn from religious and scientific interpretations, presented blacks as genetically and Biblically inferior, they were not regarded as diseased. That particular form of Southern intimacy could not have borne that burden. There was, however, another form of intimacy that thrived: despite draconian anti-miscegenation laws, white men frequently had sexual relations with black women. The taboo, however, was rigidly, even murderously, enforced between white women and black men.

Whatever the nature of sympathetic similarities and differences, the unspoken alliance of state-supported despotic practices only lasted from 1933 to 1941. Brethren in racist beliefs, the South and Nazi Germany became self-defeating partners in racial crimes. Their fates intertwined first in the heyday of their punishing racist regimes and, finally, in their demise. When Germany declared war on America in December 1941, Hitler unwittingly set in motion the ultimate unraveling of the two racial states. The United States started a military and ideological battle to return democracy to Europe. The rhetoric and propaganda of sacred ideals infused America's idealistic crusade in Europe—even in the South and even to the detriment of the Southern racial system.

> “While America was liberating Europe, the Federal government did not free its own black population from legal disenfranchisement and segregation.

With the outbreak of war, according to Douglas Blackmon, “President Franklin D. Roosevelt instinctively knew the second-class citizenship and violence imposed upon African-Americans would be exploited by the enemies of the United States.”[19] Taking the offensive, Roosevelt and his attorney general moved to eradicate neo-slavery, the most extreme practice of exploitation in the Southern system. Through United States attorneys, the federal government, for the first time since Reconstruction, attacked the peonage system. “It was a strange irony,” Blackmon wrote, “that after seventy-four years of hollow emancipation, the final delivery of African Americans from overt slavery and from the quiet complicity of the federal government in their servitude was precipitated only in response to the horrors perpetrated by an enemy country against its own despised minorities.”[20]

But there were severe limits to what the President and Federal government

19 Blackmon, Douglas, *Slavery By Another Name: The Re-Enslavement of Black Americans from the Civil War until World War II*, p.377.

20 Ibid, p.382.

were willing or able to do in opposing Jim Crow. While slavery was out, the essential practices of Jim Crow lived on during the war despite the concerns of President Roosevelt and others in his administration. While America was liberating Europe, the Federal government did not free its own black population from legal disenfranchisement and segregation. Despite the anti-racist rhetoric of freedom and democracy, under intense pressure from the white South President Roosevelt agreed to abide by entrenched segregation in the South and throughout the military at home and abroad. The need for Southern white males in the military trumped America's ideology of liberation in Europe. The power of Southern Democrats, essential to implement Roosevelt's wartime plans, effectively blocked any legislative efforts in the Congress to weaken Jim Crow. Despite intense efforts, blacks were forced to fight in segregated military units. (Blacks were even ineligible to fly planes for the Army Air Corps. The policy changed in 1941 when black pilots formed a special squadron known as the Tuskegee Airmen who later provided indispensable support for attacks on Italy and Germany.) As much as black leaders tried to link their cause with America's democratic war against Germany, neither they nor black soldiers could gain equal treatment in return for loyalty, sacrifice and value to the country.

Even after the Allied victory in 1945—a victory strongly dependent on the ideology of liberation—the status quo in the racist South seemed relatively safe and intact. Southern blacks went back to living in the despotic world of Jim Crow as well as crippling discrimination and hostility in the North. The black population was still mainly based in the South, although vast numbers had moved to find jobs in the industrial North and Mid-West in the '30s and during the war. In fact, discrimination persisted and even intensified nationwide when black veterans were denied the generous federal benefits to education, housing and medical care that were bestowed upon white veterans.

In 1948, President Truman presented the country with the stark disparity between American ideals and the reality of race in America, especially in the South. In the country that became home to the United Nations, driven by America's idealistic war and post-war aims, the President tried to act. He asked Congress to enact civil rights legislation to break the hold of Jim Crow: to end wanton killings by lynching; erase state laws and local practices that kept blacks from voting; and prevent discrimination and segregation in work and travel. No American President had ever taken such a bold initiative. "Not all groups are free to live and work," Truman wrote, "where they please or to improve their conditions of life by their own efforts. Not all groups enjoy the full privileges of citizenship.... The Federal Government has a clear duty to see that the Constitutional guarantees of individual liberties and of equal protection under the laws are not denied or abridged anywhere in the Union."[21] The Southern-dominated Congress blocked his proposals.

The continuation of racial separation in the South was in sharp contrast to America's response to the reconstruction of the German state and the birth of

21 McCullough, David, *Truman*, p. 587.

international legal accords and institutions including the United Nations, the Universal Declaration of Human Rights and the Convention on Genocide. The triumphant Allied countries imposed democracy upon West Germany and forced it to assume severe measures of responsibility for mass atrocities throughout the lands the Nazis had occupied and, most particularly, for genocide against European Jewry. Starting with the Nuremberg Trials German perpetrators of genocide were brought to account for committing crimes against humanity.

In 1945 as the Allies deliberated over bringing Nazi leaders to trial an underlying connection between the Jim Crow South and Nazi Germany emerged. The justification for prosecuting German leaders was carefully and explicitly worked out. They were to be tried for committing atrocities against the Jews as part of the expansive European war. Robert Jackson, the chief American participant in the deliberation of the Allies, made clear that nations did not have the right to interfere in the internal affairs of other nations, especially in regard to minorities. The German war against the Jews, however, extended beyond its boarders. "The reason," Jackson stated, "that this program of extermination of Jews and destruction of the rights of minorities becomes an international concern is this: it was part of a plan for making an illegal war."

Jackson protectively separated the Southern racial system from the Nazi state: "Ordinarily we do not consider that the acts of a government towards its own citizens warrant our interference. We have some regrettable circumstances at times in our own country in which minorities are unfairly treated. We think it is justifiable that we interfere or attempt to bring retribution to individuals or to states only because the concentration camps and the deportations were in pursuance of a common plan or enterprise of making an unjust or illegal war in which we became involved."[22]

Over several decades, trials, restitution payments and reeducation policies were required of the West German government. Meeting the demands of the Western Allied countries, the new German government quickly and thoroughly denounced eugenics, racial theories, anti-Semitism and the cult of the leader. The international community in the West continued to watch Germany vigilantly, although America often wavered and surreptitiously allowed many Nazis to escape prosecution in an effort to fight the Cold War. The compensatory actions of the Federal Republic, notwithstanding, most Germans sought to pass over the Nazi period and thoroughly immerse themselves in rebuilding the country's economic structure and democratic practices. It was only in the 1960s that younger generations in Germany boldly confronted their national history of genocide and prevailed over the silence of their parents.

The 1960s were the critical turning point for the South as well. A massive movement of unrelenting protest, led by black Americans, forced the federal government finally to employ its power to destroy Jim Crow. The pressure had

22 Huhle, Rainer, Ed. *Human Rights and History: A Challenge for Education*, (EVZ Foundation), pp. 56-57.

been building irresistibly over two decades. "Thousands of African American men," Blackmon wrote, "who returned as fighting men, unwilling to capitulate again to the docile state of helplessness that preceded the war, abandoned the South altogether or joined in the agitation that would become the civil rights movement."[23] That movement required the unraveling of Jim Crow and the radical reworking of Southern society—the dismantling of the traditional racial culture of established relationships, official laws, prevailing habits and deep-seated attitudes of fear and hierarchy. The change had to take place in the epicenter of a mixed society but the pressures for change were overwhelming.

They came from within and without—from inside America's closed world of Jim Crow and outside from the broad currents of international events. Despite the fact that discrimination against blacks was national in scope, it was Jim Crow—the racial system—that challenged the validity of American power and its democratic leadership. (Only, South Africa and Rhodesia served as kindred racial states in the 1950s and early 1960s.) Under scrutiny from the rest of the world in the contest for allies in the Cold War, America could no longer separate a race ridden-South from the rest of the country.

From the end of the war until the triumph of the Civil Rights movement, the white population had resisted the pressures to abandon its white privileges and superiority based on homegrown legality and violence. The first significant break came through President Truman's leadership when he ordered an end to segregation in the army in 1947. Enforcement was painfully slow. Year after year, opponents of Jim Crow worked laboriously through the courts to force the federal judiciary to invalidate segregation in its most glaring forms. Brown v. Board of Education was the first great victory in 1954. But it was not until the 1960s that the full force of protests by courageous black individuals, such as Martin Luther King and John Lewis, groups and movements—state by state, city by city, school by school, street by street, and bridge by bridge—destroyed the official edifice of Jim Crow. Only then did America begin to realize the promise of the 13th, 14th and 15th Amendments to the US Constitution passed in the aftermath of the Civil War.

The slow, tangled retreat from Jim Crow—both peaceful and violent—took place in America's heterogeneous society through heroic civil resistance, political and legal confrontations. In Germany, in the absence of a Jewish population, the post-war country's recovery from its racist past occurred within a homogenous population. In the aftermath of the Second World War and the defeat of National Socialism, West Germany, starting first with occupation, was condemned through scorn and heavy moral and financial debts. Post Jim Crow, the Southern political system was radically changed but powerful strains of racial discrimination persisted in the interstices of the South and country as a whole.

The Nazi racial state remains the subject of international scrutiny and condemnation. In Europe and the US, National Socialism continues to be the

23 Blackmon, p.381.

supreme example of the violation of human rights and the dangers of racism and xenophobia. In the Western world, Germany under Hitler still provides the extreme and most abhorrent example of criminality and racial destruction on a massive scale. *The Diary of Anne Frank*, Elie Wiesel's *Night*, Claude Lanzmann's "Shoah," and the funeral site of Auschwitz-Birkenau are part of the cultural and historical canon of responsibility in the Western world. "Never again," the slogan of moral and political redemption is not just for Germany, but also for Europe as a whole.

As the conclusion of his epic work on post-war Europe, Tony Judt affirmed: "The Holocaust today is much more than just another undeniable fact about a past that Europeans can no longer choose to ignore. As Europe prepares to leave World War Two behind—as the last memorials are inaugurated, the last surviving combatants and victims honored—the recovered memory of Europe's dead Jews has become the very definition and guarantee of the continent's restored humanity."[24] It is a European obligation. Nonetheless, Germany's war and ultimate defeat have placed the country in a category of its own.

America, too, is in a category of its own, but one characterized by certain exceptions and evasions. No such burden for "restored humanity" is placed on America and particularly the American South. There is no question that significant and long-awaited progress has been made since the Civil Rights movement through the expansion of a black middle class, acceptance of blacks in the highest judicial, corporate and political ranks, culminating with the election of President Barak Obama. But no nations including America have forced the South (or the broader population) to repudiate thoroughly its racist past, reeducate its populations on racial issues and acknowledge in real or symbolic ways the financial and cultural impoverishment of blacks subjected to slavery, Jim Crow and ongoing discrimination and prejudice. However broadly read and honored, no works of literature such as Invisible Man, by Ralph Ellison, the works of W.E.B. Du Bois, the biography W. E. B. Du Bois, by David Levering Lewis or historical studies such as Parting the Waters, by Taylor Branch, have captured the imagination or hearts of a vast public to provide one means of reconciliation with the past.

The universal human rights discourse attempts to understand terms such as collaborators, bystanders, perpetrators, indifference, passivity, complicity, genocide, mass atrocities and persecution on racial, ethnic and religious grounds. But American slavery and segregation are frequently exempt from this discussion. The specific vocabulary is not usually applied and often rejected outright. What explains the vast difference in regard to terminology and accountability? One must ask whether there is a strain of American exceptionalism and superiority—based on pervasive myths of equality and opportunity—that discourages America from connecting its history of racism and repudiating that past with that of another racist state.

The question needs to be addressed as part of a renewed international dialogue to confront ongoing dangers of racial, ethnic and religious tensions animosities and

24 Judt, Tony, *Postwar*, p.804.

the underground persistence of racist beliefs. Europe faces challenges through the unanticipated emergence of diverse populations and mutations of anti-Semitism, while America continues to face the insidious persistence of prejudice against its black and immigrant populations –especially immigrants of color. Once again, immigrants on both continents are being thrown into a corrosive no-man's land of not belonging and subject to the vituperative language of extremist politicians and their supporters.

The histories of the German and Southern racial systems set side-by-side present warnings. They shared complementary beliefs and policies, although the German system lasted hardly a generation; the American survived through centuries of slavery and segregation through policies, behaviors and beliefs that deeply infused the culture of the region. One system ended relatively quickly in shattering defeat and the suicide of its leader; the other, despite military failure, years of occupation, and three egalitarian amendments to the Constitution, persisted for nearly a century after Lee's surrender at Appomattox and only gradually yielded to unrelenting insistence on civil rights for blacks and all Americans.

The German government regards its years of outright racial wars with inexorable guilt, while the white South, with the sympathetic support of the Republican Party, often celebrates its Confederate and pre-civil rights past with heroic pride and nostalgia. In 2011, one hundred and fifty years after secession and the start of the Civil War, many Southern states celebrated the date with balls and festivities. In distinct contrast, it is unimaginable that any reputable German political or social leaders could honor and commemorate the passage of the Nuremberg Laws and the erection of a German racist state.

The consequences of accountability and reconciliation with a grievous past continue to influence contemporary events and attitudes in Germany and America. Whatever the differences and similarities, there should be no escape from the fact that these two racial states affected the 20th Century in disastrous ways. Confronting the histories and legacies of the racial abyss—legacies that underlie current discourse and behavior—remains imperative for both societies, especially for their younger generations, in the 21st Century as well.

Jan Karski and Stefan Zweig

Remarks to the Humanity in Action Fourth International Conference, June 2013

This conference in Warsaw is a dream come true. Over the past three years, the annual Humanity in Action conferences have taken place in Amsterdam, Berlin and Sarajevo. Each time we considered where to hold the conference, Monika and Magda invited us to go east. And now, thanks to their phenomenal work along with Phil and Antje, we are here in this vibrant country and city to probe into various fascinating aspects of Polish history in the 20th and 21st centuries. This inquiry is valuable not just for the history of transitions and the restoration of a democratic state but for the promise of Poland as a new center of European culture as Western Europe looks increasingly to the needs of Central and Eastern Europe.

It is an honor to be at this extraordinary and stunning Jewish Museum, even before it officially opens. We are most grateful to the Director Andrzej Cudak and Jan Spievak, a Senior Fellows, who have made this happen.

We started the Humanity in Action Polish program seven years ago under the guidance of Humanity in Action Germany and with the singularly generous support of the German Foundation Remembrance, Responsibility and Future (EVZ). This expansion has stretched our boundaries and horizons in numerous challenging ways, mainly in regard to diversity issues. This requires a short explanation. Among the many countries that are part of the Humanity in Action, Poland today has the least ethnic, racial and religious diversity. Before the Second World War, however, it was the most diverse. Thus, the temptation to throw ourselves back and concentrate on the disastrous history of the war years, to grapple with the so called vanished limb of diversity, particularly in regard to Polish Jewry. Thanks to the insightful and creative programmatic work of Monika and Magda, that past is only one substantial part of the subjects they take on. Thus, the Fellows explore how Poland has resisted and recovered from totalitarian regimes; how it strengthened its democratic processes; how it battles to reduce discrimination against the disabled and gays; how it organizes social campaigns; and how it impresses the Polish voice upon the European and transatlantic discourse.

Our dear friend Konstanty Gebert has said that Poland has too much history to absorb. I am sure he is right but I am afraid as an historian, I can't resist the temptation to think first in historical terms. Thus, I wish to speak about two people who can illuminate our present challenges: Jan Karski, the Polish resistance fighter and illustrious professor of international relations at Georgetown University in Washington, DC and Stefan Zweig, still widely read in Germany and Austria as a significant novelist, dramatist and biographer but unfortunately less known today in America.

A few years ago Claude Lanzmann published his autobiography, *The Patagonian Hare*. Lanzmann is best known for making the film "Shoah" (and having an affair with Simon de Beauvoir). The book is fascinating, long, often funny, insightful and a great example of his irrepressible narcissistic drive. In the climatic portion about making "Shoah" Lanzmann mentioned that he did three interviews with Jan Karski that were not in the film. Having read *The Secret State*, Karski's remarkable book published in 1944, I was eager to see the interviews on YouTube.

I would like to share two segments with you because I think they are so moving and historically informative. The Polish underground movement to which he belonged sent Karski to England and the US in 1942 and 1943. His mission was to give first hand accounts of the resistance in Poland to the German occupation and generate confidence in a post-war democratic Poland—the "secret state" in formation. He was also tasked with informing officials and various leaders in England and the US about the fate of Polish Jewry. Thus, Karski a young Catholic was surreptitiously brought into the Warsaw ghetto in 1942 and in the uniform of a guard to Izbica, (not Belzec as he states in the interview) a transit camp that employed gas to kill Jews.

In the first interview Karski described his meeting with President Roosevelt in the White House in 1943, one that was arranged by the Polish Ambassador to the United States. The context is pretty clear: Karski was to bring first-hand testimony to the President to solicit his support for protecting Polish democratic interests against the Germans as well as pressures from internal and external Communist forces. The context for the second video segment is more complicated. Karski described his meeting with Szmul Zygielbojm in a London office. Zygielbojm was a member of the Polish National Council and the Bund, a Jewish political party with Socialist leanings that was active in pre-war Poland.

After watching the two interviews I was struck by the historic importance of the two voices: the dramatic disparities in power and personality between Roosevelt and Zygielbojm and Karski's radically different reactions to the two men. They personify opposite extremes of authority and emotion. The President was cool, commanding, immobile due to his paralyzed legs, in total control of the conversation—and seemingly in control of the fate of a Polish democratic state. Karski was in awe of the President's power and stunningly aware of the constrained and inflexible borders of the President's interest in Poland and Polish Jewry. The messenger clearly understood that he would not propel the President to strong supportive action for the Polish resistance, a democratic state or Polish Jews.

Zygielbojm in London reacted in a totally different way. Overcome by emotion, he was agitated, distraught by his helplessness, nearly hysterical and despairing of finding ways to inform the world and those in power of what was happening to Polish Jews. In this case, Karski knew that Zygielbojm completely understood the searing news of massive destruction in Poland. A few weeks later, Zygeilbojm spoke passionately on the BBC: "It will actually be a shame to go on living, to belong to the human race if steps are not taken to halt the greatest crime in human history."[25] In May 1943 Zygeilbojm committed suicide after once more asking, in a final note, that the world take action.

In 1944 Karski published his first book *The Secret State*. He wrote for an American audience in compelling detail about his history as a young, little known resistance fighter, his visits to England and the US, his meetings with the President and leaders of the Jewish community in the West and his fervent hopes for the reestablishment of a Polish democratic state. They were unfulfilled. He did not return to Poland but instead became a professor in Washington DC and an expert on Communism and international relations. And, according to his testimony as recorded in his conversation with Lanzmann, despite his role and first-hand knowledge, he confessed that he never taught or discussed for the next 40 years what had happened to Polish Jewry in the Holocaust. This courageous man, could not do it, he could not talk about it. He had no more messages to share about what happened. He kept his grief to himself. In a certain sense, this powerful history, formed by a resistance fighter, democrat, forthright observer and bold messenger, is one of silence—a silence that reverberates with profound meaning and poignancy.

Stefan Zweig embodies another kind of silence that is equally powerful and sad. In 1941, he was close to completing an expansive, semi-autobiography work, *The World of Yesterday*. And again like Karski, he wrote parts of the work as a foreigner in the States. Unlike Karski, however, Zweig drew upon his literary skills as a famous European author of remarkable productivity, quality and critical success with translations in over 30 languages. He was at one point the best selling author in Europe—as novelist, biographer, dramatist and essayist. His family roots were in Galicia, a part of Poland that was taken over by the Hapsburgs in the late 18th Century. Zweig's family escaped the densely populated and insular Galician Jewish world and migrated to the thriving Austrian capitol. His father prospered as a businessman enabling his son to grow up in secure affluence, to shun the family business for a literary career. Zweig joined the Viennese and European liberal intelligentsia establishing close friendships with great figures such as Sigmund Freud, Paul Valery, Richard Strauss, James Joyce, Arturo Toscanini and many others. As an established writer, he enriched the vibrant, audacious cosmopolitan Viennese society that transformed art, science, music, theatre and literature in the late 19th and early 20th centuries. Until the First World War, he felt that he lived at the center of creativity and freedom.

The World of Yesterday is a powerful evocation of thwarted aspirations for the Europe

25 Wood, E, Thomas and Janowski, Stanislaw M.Karski: *How One Man Tried to Stop the Holocaust*. p. 152.

of his youth—regret for the lost hope of a liberal, harmonious, democratic Europe—and a furious indictment of dictatorial and mass violence. The work, imbued with a modesty that Lanzmann could never dream of, describes Zweig's pre-World War I hopes, as a pacifist, for a united, peaceful, inclusive, humanist European society. They failed: first through the nationalistic aggressions that fueld the First World War, then the fall of the Hapsburg Empire and ensuing years of economic chaos after the conflict ended. When Europe seemed to return to normalcy in the '20s, Zweig reignited his dreams for a peaceful future and a united European culture. Hitler shattered any such possibilities starting in the early 1930s. Zweig's books were burned and then banned in Germany. In 1934, Austria was no longer safe for him. He emigrated to England. Within a few years, his writings were banned in every country that Germany conquered and his broad circles of intellects and democrats were in flight. While he had voluntarily left for England in the mid-30s, with the Anschluss, Zweig lost his citizenship and became a refugee, stripped of his nationality, culture and home.

"I believe that being in Poland today, a country that has gone through too many purgatories and hells, affirms the fervent democratic beliefs of both Karksi and Zweig.

In Bath, England on September 1, 1939, Zweig sought to obtain a marriage license to marry for a second time. He went to the registry office to sign papers. "Just then—it must have been about eleven o'clock—the door to the next room flew open. A young official burst in, getting into his coat while walking. 'The Germans have invaded Poland. This is war,' he shouted into the quiet room. The word fell like a hammer blow upon my heart,"[26] Zweig wrote. As an Austrian by birth, he knew he would immediately become an enemy alien in England. "Again I was aware that the past was done for, work achieved was in ruins, Europe, our home, to which we had dedicated ourselves, had suffered a destruction that would extend far beyond our life. Something new, a new world began, but how many hells, how many purgatories had to be crossed before it could be reached."[27]

Zweig had spent the years since leaving Austria in England, the US and finally Brazil. It was there that he and his wife jointly committed suicide in 1942. In the final passages of *The World of Yesterday*, he wrote of shadows: first watching his own, as he walked down a sunny street in London right after England declared war on Germany and then the gloomy shadow of the First World War which he thought might suffuse his autobiography. "But, after all, shadows themselves are born of light. And only he who has experienced dawn and dusk, war and peace, ascent and decline, only he has truly lived."[28]

I believe that being in Poland today, a country that has gone through too many

26 Zweig, Stephen, *The World of Yesterday*, p. 459.

27 Ibid, p. 462.

28 Ibid, p. 462.

purgatories and hells, affirms the fervent democratic beliefs of both Karksi and Zweig. Although pessimism and despair drove Zweig to suicide, the act did not invalidate his hopes for a peaceful and a humane European existence. Karski built a new life in America and waited for the fall of the Communist regime. There is probably too much history in Poland to digest, as Konstanty Gebert says. But it is only by bringing that history into the present and searching for knowledge, meaning, and idealistic, humanistic beliefs that we can meet our responsibilities to the present and future. Might I say that in speaking of "we," I mean to speak principally to those in Humanity in Action. We are obligated individually and collectively to avoid silence. We seek to understand the present through the past. At this conference and through the annual Polish Humanity in Action programs, we seek to gain greater exposure to and understanding of the brilliant intellectual tradition of historical research that belongs to Poland. We seek to encounter great figures from the past, such as Karski and Zweig, who inform us about their lives and times—times that still deeply affect the boundaries of our challenges, needs and hopes in Europe and the United States. We seek to draw wisdom and courage from their courage and values.

In seeking wisdom we turn to the great Polish poet Czeslow Milosz. His Polish voice—truly a universal voice which meshes with those of Karksi and Zweig—illuminates our presence in Warsaw today and the painful challenges of past and present that we assume.

> Still one more year of preparation.
> Tomorrow at the latest I will start working on a great book
> In which my country will appear as it really was.
> The sun will rise over the wise and wicked.
> Springs and autumns will unerringly return,
> In a wet thicket a thrush will build his nest lined with clay
> And foxes will learn their foxy natures.
>
> And that will be the subject, with addenda. Thus, armies
> Running across frozen plains, shouting a curse
> In a many-voiced chorus; the cannon of a tank
> Growing immense at the corner of a street; the ride at dusk
> Into a camp with watchtowers and barbed wire.
>
> No, it won't happen tomorrow. In five or ten years.
> I still think too much about the mothers
> And ask what is man born of women.
> He curls himself up and protects his head
> While he is kicked by heavy boots; on fire and running,
> He burns with bright flame; a bulldozer sweeps him into clay pit.
> Her child. Embracing a teddy bear. Conceived in ecstasy.
> I haven't learned yet to speak as I should, calmly.[29]

29 Milosz, Czeslaw, *Unattainable Earth*, p.61.

The Flight and Rescue of Danish Jewry

Talk at the Conference "Civil Resistance and the Holocaust," Copenhagen, October 2013

We are most grateful to the Danish Humanity in Action Board of Directors, led by Anders Jerichow and the staff who conceived of and organized this extraordinary conference. For me there is a sense of full and deep appreciation as well as partial fulfillment. Over 18 years ago, I asked Herbert Pundik if we could put together a program for university students in Denmark and the United States to try to understand the rescue of Jews in Denmark. He said yes, although I believe he secretly harbored some skepticism as to weather we would really do a credible job. Nonetheless, we promised each other—I mean I promised him and he almost believed me—that this would not be some adventure in creating simplistic explanations that would further embellish contorted legends and myths. We intended to deal with complexities, right from the beginning. This conference is an impressive result of all the work that the Danish Humanity in Action Fellows, board and staff have done over 15 years under the leadership of Herbert Pundik, Uffe Stormgaard and Anders Jerichow.

But there is also a sense of incomplete and partial fulfillment. Even today, 70 years after the flight and rescue of Danish Jewry, there are still difficulties in understanding the complex and complete history: the expectations and ambiguous actions of German occupiers at different levels of authority and power; the knowledge, actions, and values of Danish Christians working from different positions and locations in the country; the fearful and often chaotic responses of Danish Jews and immigrant Jews in Denmark to the dangers of German anti-Semitism.

Nevertheless, in the ensuring years we have accumulated knowledge and memories to form the history of a unique and, in the context of the Holocaust, a miraculous escape that sustained the Jewish community and enabled it to return to Denmark, almost intact, in 1945. I refrain from using the word heroic because the Danes have an aversion to the concept. But unique and miraculous are fully justified despite the betrayals and greed of some Danes in regard to the Jews. No other country, qua country, meaning civil servants and significant parts of the population, protected their Jewish countrymen from German racial hatred, degradation, starvation, violence and death. The Danish response was so unusual that it almost seems miraculous. The word evokes many meanings such as supernatural and magical. I don't use it in those ways. Instead, remarkable and extraordinary provide the appropriate meanings.

I would suggest, following the lead of Bo Lidegaard, that rescue was built upon shared moral values—expressed most significantly through the development of the welfare state—that had entered the fiber of thousands of Danish individual and the collectivity.[30] When tested by the Germans, accepting Jews as Danes was the decent thing to do; protecting Jews as a means of finally and openly resisting the Germans was a redemptive thing to do; accepting Jews as equally valuable human beings was the Christian thing to do.

In 1989 Saul Friedlander, one of the great historians of Nazi Germany and the Holocaust, wrote his autobiography *When Memory Comes*. His family, assimilated Jews from Prague, escaped to France in the late 30s. With the German invasion in 1940 they fled into the French countryside. He recalled his sick father in 1941 living in a "sort of wordless sadness," having chosen not to flee to Sweden or Palestine, away from Hitler, as did other members of the family. "What could my father have done? Nothing depended on him now. A safer hiding place depended on the good will of others, as did fleeing the country. Rebellion had no meaning for the few scattered Jews who saw the vise closing. Whom would they attack?" And thus the tragedy of his father and mother who were deported. "...my father was hunted down for what he had refused to remain: a Jew. What he wanted to become, a man like others, had been taken away from him, leaving him no possible recourse. He was being refused the right to live and no longer even knew what to die for. Much more than the impossibility of acting, his desperate straits had become an impossibility of living."[31]

“When tested by the Germans, accepting Jews as Danes was the decent thing to do; protecting Jews as a means of finally and openly resisting the Germans was a redemptive thing to do; accepting Jews as equally valuable human beings was the Christian thing to do.

The Danish Jews were different but only because of other Danish people. Like Friedlander's father, Danish Jews, many of them assimilated, were passive, lulled into believing they would be spared, afraid to act. But they could turn to others or others, significantly, knew how to turn to them; they could follow the lead of protectors, there was a way to escape to Sweden. This is the memory that Jews hold; this is the history that gives honor to the Danish people.

But what does that history mean today? What is the relevance? What are the conceptual tools we, Humanity in Action and a broader public, need to find

30 Lidegaard, Bo, Countrymen.

31 Friedlander, Saul, *When Memory Comes*, pp. 55-56.

to sustain this history? The time for recalling memories, however painful and incomplete, is just about over. Those like Friedlander who took years to unlock the past and try to understand, have done their work. We can no longer depend upon the impact of personal connections to that past.

I would like to suggest that we continue to seek to understand that history in the context of resilience and resistance. In fact, this was a founding precept of Humanity in Action. Resilience and resistance are usually discussed in terms of trauma, particular for children who have experienced abuse and for victims or soldiers in war. (There is also a growing body of literature and studies relating these ideas to business and individual entrepreneurship.) Resilience and resistance are concepts that relate not only to individual responses but also embrace collective action—trusting others, working together towards shared goals with common values, drawing upon the resources and strengths of many people. Resilience and resistance through collective action and the action of civil society need to inform contemporary challenges where we encounter circumstances of loss and calamity—whether it be in the destruction of our environments; seemingly irresolvable conflicts in the Middle East and Africa; and the inadequacies of our economic systems that fail to provide basic needs for our societies, particularly in the United States and other places throughout the world.

In April 1940 Denmark was a failed state—a society that accepted immediate military defeat at the hands of the Germans and the charade of democratic self-government. In fact, the Danish government, according to Bo Lidegaard, anticipated occupation long before it happened. It expected to lose. It negotiated and cooperated with the Germans and met the German demands as the so-called "model protectorate" in order to keep the Germans from destroying the country and installing a violently repressive Nazi driven regime. For three years the Danish government succumbed and gave no support to the small Danish resistance movement.

Not everyone, however, gave up completely, especially small groups in resistance organizations and Henrik Kauffmann the audacious Danish Ambassador to the United States. Finally, the country recovered its bearings in the late summer of 1943 after the Danish government refused to execute resistance fighters. Danes found the means to act upon the values of decency and social responsibility—cooperative action in supporting a minority—that were the foundation of the welfare state developed in the previous decades. National resistance through individual and collective action gained strength in the fall of 1943 when thousands upon thousands of Danes protected the Jews, facilitated their escape to Sweden, sheltered their homes and assets while in exile and welcomed them back to Denmark after the end of the war.

The history, as this conference reveals, is deeply complicated and nuanced. It is clear that there was much suffering and in too many Danish quarters complicity with the Germans. The rescue was not purely altruistic, as romanticized especially by Americans. Danish Jews who were captured and sent to Theresienstadt suffered deeply, during the War and for decades after. They mostly kept the traumas embedded in themselves, ever thankful for the sustenance they received—food, clothing and vitamins sent from Demark; ever thankful for the understanding worked out between Werner Best and Aldolf Eichmann, that they would not be sent farther east to an extermination camp; ever thankful for liberation from the camp by the Danish and Swedish Red Cross a month before the end of the war; ever thankful that they were the exception, as our esteemed Rabbi Bent Melchior, has said: it is customary for Jews to be expelled but rarely, ever so rarely, to be embraced when they return from expulsion.

Danish civil servants and organizations assumed responsibility to protect the Danish Jews deported to Theresienstadt. How extraordinary: beyond the Danish borders, the Jews were still Danes. This was defiance, resilience and resistance to despicable Fascist actions and beliefs—all in the Danish spirit of collective values and behaviors. Thus, despite the bystanders and collaborators, this unique national model of resilience and resistance still serves as an example of collective action, based upon shared values that saved a threatened minority. "...humans are human only," Claude Lanzmann wrote in his autobiography *The Patagonian Hare*, "because they have the capacity to transform that which oppresses them into something of value, and to sacrifice themselves for it. It is the very essence of humanity, but could also be called tradition, or even more, culture."[32] In the Danish case it was both the liberal Christian "tradition" and the "culture" of social responsibility.

There is still much to learn and make relevant to our contemporary challenges. Humanity in Action remains committed to the premise that Herbert Pundik agreed to in 1997: let us probe with diligent and objectivity Denmark's complex and unique history during the war and the Holocaust and commend the history of individual and collective resilience and resistance that remains deeply meaningful. And let us continue to do it by collective international inquiry that enhances the ever-growing Humanity in Action community of people engaged in promoting democracy, justice, historical knowledge and the public good.

32 Lanzmann, Claude, *The Patagonian Hare*, pp. 312-313.

The Journal of Helene Berr

Talk with Humanity in Action Fellows, Paris, June 2010

A few months ago I read *The Journal of Helene Berr* that I have recommended that you all read. I wanted to make it obligatory reading for you but we didn't have the time or resources to get the book into all of your hands. Some of you may have read it but I suspect most have not done so yet. Let me urge you to read this extraordinary work.

Helene Berr lived in Paris for most of her life. Written at home, the journal extends from 1940 to 1944 when she was arrested. She did not intend to provide a meticulous documentation of the descent into madness and violence under occupation. Her entries start sparsely, seemingly superficial and incidental, but grow to evoke the power and depth of a great orchestral work that draws from many different themes and rhythms into climax and denouement.

Its power derives from a poignant innocence, a testing of the method of communicating with herself, an ability to draw upon her resources in literature and philosophy to provide strength to face the unprecedented and unanticipated changes in her life.

Without one ounce of self-pity she described the following. What it meant to love her Parisian family, home and surroundings—friends, streets, apartments, university, stores, villages, country houses—and then see that world metastasize into zones of persecution and violence. What it was like to fall in love, to be deprived of the strength and support of someone who had joined the resistance movement and whom she would probably never see again. What it meant to lose the confidence in public spaces that once gave opportunity, education, adventure, enjoyment—to feel the security of her bourgeois existence cascade down into peril and torment. What it meant to be cast into the dire world of innocent victim based upon religious and pseudo-racial differentiation. What it meant to decide between resistance and flight. What it meant to recognize the defilement and danger that would attend deportation to the East and the certain early end to her life.

Let me read a few excerpts.

Wednesday, November 24, 1943

"This morning I was reading Shelley and his *Defense of Poetry*, yesterday evening, one of the dialogues of Plato that he translated. How desperate to think that all this, all these magnificent fruits of refinement and humanism, all that intelligence and breadth of mind, are dead. To live in times like these and be drawn to all these works is absurd, it's almost incompatible. What would Plato have said? What would Shelley say? They'd tell me I was a useless dreamer. But surely what is false and wrong are other people and tide of rabid evil sweeping through the world. Had I been born in another time, it would all have been able to blossom."[33]

Monday, December 13, 1943

"Today, at the English Department, Lucie Morizet stayed behind on purpose to wait for me...to tell me that one of her friends had told her to warn all her friends of our kind that they would be taken before December 31. She was adamant I should do something. Do what? I'd have to lift a whole planet."[34]

Friday, December 31, 1943

"When I write the word *Jew*, I am not saying exactly what I mean, because for me that distinction does not exist: I do not feel different from other people, I will never think of myself as a member of a separate human group, and perhaps that is why I suffer so much, because I do not understand it at all. I suffer from the spectacle of human beastliness. I suffer from the sight of evil falling on humanity; but as I do not feel I belong to any particular racial, religious, or human group (because such a feeling always implies pride), all I have to keep me going are my inner debates and reactions, my conscience."[35]

In the early 1940s, the immediate world of Helene Berr was Paris, although, in many of her later passages, the horizon spread ominously to the East. This "planet," as she imaginatively viewed the world, was totally beyond her scope and reach. Today our concepts and knowledge are totally different. In our world the reality of the planet has become much more immediate, accessible and subject to our control. We have unprecedented scope and resources for improving and degrading—sometimes both at the same time—our existence. What responsibilities we have called upon ourselves! What challenges we confront!

Where does Humanity in Action fit into this world of global tests and trials? Our focus is on the critical and often fragile intersections of diversity and human rights. Our boundaries encompass the national and international, the individual and his or her network, the past and present. We call for engagement through collaborative efforts to sustain a world of just values and behaviors that differ radically from the destructive spirit and forces that overtook the life of Helene Berr.

33 Helene Berr, *The Journal of Helene Berr*, p. 218.

34 Ibid, p. 229.

35 Ibid. p. 236.

On Wednesday, January 24, 1944, Helene wrote: "What a shame that one half of humanity in *manufacturing evil* and a tiny minority is trying to put it right." We hope and expect that all of you belong to that "minority." We know that it most probably will always be a minority, but let it always be an expanding network committed to putting it "right."[36]

36 Ibid, p. 246.

Religion and Human Rights in Europe

March 15, 2005

This past Sunday Francis Fukuyama published an article in the Book Review section of the *New York Times* about the relevance of Max Weber's *The Protestant Ethic and the Spirit of Capitalism*. Fukuyama observed: "Europe today is a continent that is peaceful, prosperous, rationally administered by the European Union and thoroughly secular. Europeans may continue to use terms like "human rights" and human dignity," which are rooted in the Christian values of their civilization, but few of them could give a coherent account of why they continue to believe in such things. The host of dead religious beliefs haunts Europe much more than it does American."[37]

There is no reason to expect that Fukuyama would or should have written more expansively about the nature of religion in Europe today since his perspective was singularly focused on Protestant beliefs, economics, culture and society. But I found his paragraph to be interesting because he identifies Europe as "peaceful," secular and secularly committed to the doctrine of human rights—and religiously dead. Yes, Europe is at peace under America's protective shield. Yes, Europe abhors war, especially American induced wars, and wishes and believes that negotiations and reason will defuse just about any conflict.

Europe, no longer prone to making war on its own continent, feels at peace with the rest of the world. But Europe, and in this context I speak mainly about Western Europe, is not at peace with itself. I think that this is mainly due to the religious challenge posed by millions of Muslims and Arabs within Europe's borders. In France, the Muslim/Arab population is somewhere between 4 and 5 million out of 60 millions; in Denmark, 200,000 out of 5 million; in The Netherlands over 1,000,000 out of 16 million and in Germany 3 million out of a total population of 80 million. The Muslim and Arab populations have grown in Europe as a result of European guest worker policies in the 1960s, family unification policies, liberal asylum procedures, open borders for former colonial subjects in countries such as France and the spectacularly higher birth rates of the immigrants compared to the

37 *New York Times*, March 13, 2005, p.35.

host European populations.

One doesn't have to be in Europe to know that many European countries are having a hard time coming to terms living with their non-Christian populations—and I would include its Jewish populations as part of changing perceptions and attitudes about other religious minorities. In the American media, one reads stories almost everyday about these difficulties. To cite but a few stories that recently appeared in the *Times*. Two Dutch parliamentarians, one a Muslim who castigates certain Muslim practices and the other a Christian who campaigns against allowing more immigrants in to The Netherlands, have to be guarded all the time because of death treats. (A segment on "60 Minutes" featured Hirshi Ali one of those two under constant threat.) British moderate Muslims are trying to gain a stronger voice over that of British extremists; The Mayor of London pronounced that Israel is engaged in ethnic cleaning and that Sharon is a war criminal; disputes over Muslim women wearing the veil at schools and at work; French prisons as breeding grounds for extremist views. These subjects constitute a small sampling from the media.

The European and American press have woken up to these issues. Politicians are forced to take positions about immigration and refugee policies. And private views of suspicions and discomfort are spilling into public discourse despite the armature of political correctness and restrictive notions of free speech—restrictive, that is, compared to America's dedication to the First Amendment.

Every European country is different in its history, current political discourse and configurations of political forces that affect religious and other majority/minority issues. But every European country faces the traumatic fact that it—the nation state—is no longer homogeneous racially, religiously and ethnically as it was after the Second World War. Every Western European country, also shares the common legacy of having accepted human rights principles and institutions in the reckoning after War and Holocaust. Human rights doctrines and institutions developed as a means of moral rectification in Europe and, in America, as the idealistic justification for defeating the Axis countries. Western Europe started anew in the sphere of universal values and norms after it had destroyed itself through Nazi aggression and acceptance, complicity or powerlessness—or a lethal combination of all three—of anti-Semitic persecution. Furthermore, national laws put force behind the noble human rights doctrines, which were essentially a wish list of best behavior for the human population. Human rights doctrines were also deeply relevant in a tumultuous period, in the late 40s and 50s, of colonial resistance to European domination and the Cold War.

What were those human rights principles that Fukuyama says that Europeans now can't identify? They were acclaimed in the Universal Declaration of Human Rights passed in the UN's General Assembly in December 1948. It is important to remember that Europe accepted the human rights doctrines when it was essentially free of minority tensions within its own borders: European Jewry was decimated and religious affiliations and beliefs were less and less relevant to major portions of the Western European populations. Through those doctrines, Europe guarded itself against a resurgence of hatred, which it anticipated and feared would come from the right in order to protect the victims of the past. Europe never anticipated that its human rights pronouncements would be tested in regard to its Muslim and Arab populations.

The process of secularization continued during student protests of the 60s. The sexual, gender and social revolutions of that period finally pushed Christian leaders and institutions out of the mainstream. Europe was happily liberated, prosperous and buttressed by the welfare state which incorporated economic security and idealistic values. European nations committed themselves to high taxation in the service of high benefits and moral principles—soft Christianity, one could say. After the devastation of the Depression in the 30s and the War, Europe finally committed itself to taking care of its own.

If Europe loves human rights, it loves the welfare state even more. And there is the rub—or at least one part of its disaffection with the current states of affairs. The welfare state was built on a sense of sharing with one's own people—sharing benefits and values that reflected a consensus about religious identification—or lack thereof—work, family, sexual mores, gender and public and private behavior. But who constitutes "ones own" in Europe? Well, millions of people who support secular Europe built upon a Christian template. There is little ritual observance: churches are empty most of the time; many have even been converted to art centers; priests and ministers are hard to find. Yet, I think it critical to recognize that there is a residual Christianity that is alive to the perceived and real differences in regard to the Muslim and Arab populations in Europe.

"Beyond the intrinsic distrust of others, Europe has to come to terms with its diverse populations in the post 9/11 world."

The sense of the "other" goes two ways. The other, from the European Christian/secular perspective, is the Muslim and Arab population present but essentially ignored in Europe in the 1960s through the following decades. The other, from the European-based Muslim perspective, is the Christian or secular European. Those different perceptions of the other —perceived and real—are central to a multiplicity of tensions in Europe. They affect the welfare state, the nature of the family, young students, what you can say, write and film, women and men in the workplace, at university and at home. We know all too well how that sense of the other turns into prejudice, hatred, even paranoia. Studies about anger, emotions and prejudice show that humans may be inherently suspicious of those who are different. In fact, people are wired to distrust outsiders, according to some recent studies at Northwestern University.

Beyond the intrinsic distrust of others, Europe has to come to terms with its diverse populations in the post 9/11 world. Fears of terrorism rest dangerously upon Europe's obvious failures to integrate their Arab and Muslim populations. Muslims can become radicalized in Europe because of the dislocation, discrimination and the temptations of the secular life. Set adrift in Europe, the reversion to the familiar can turn easily into the religious fanaticism as a means of providing a viable identity and resistance to European society. A resurgence of anti-Semitism with its vestigial Christian roots now mixes with Muslim and Arab antagonisms towards Jews in Europe because of Israel's presence in the Arab world.

Islam appears to be a vital, immediate source of belief and identity for Muslims in Europe in contradistinction to the residual religious concerns of Europeans. Thus, when people speak of a dialogue about religions in Europe, one must move beyond Christians, Jews and Muslims to include the secularists who are the most dominant part of the population. It is obvious that discussions cannot be limited to theologians and political party that represented the interests of Protestants or Catholics, as was the case into the mid-20th century. Who speaks for the secularists? What are their beliefs? And who in Europe speaks for Islam given its decentralized nature?

Each European country will deal with the religious/secular, minority/majority dichotomies based upon its own history and political, cultural, social, secular and religious currents. Some countries, such as Britain and Sweden, are more amenable to minority populations; some, such as Denmark, are unwilling to undergo basic changes in their populations and sense of identity. It is perfectly clear, however, that one critical challenge is both nation-based and European wide: how will Europe reconcile its obligations to abide by idealistic human rights declarations with its yearning for homogeneity—yearnings that are based upon a common Christian past and current secular beliefs and behaviors.

Diplomacy and Diversity

Talk with Fellows, May 2014

Thank you, American and European Fellows, for joining this experimental program on diplomacy and pluralism at an extraordinary time of challenge in international realms. We have constructed this program in Washington and Paris to explore some of the most important issues facing us today. Our aim is to provide historical and contemporary insights from some of the very best internationally oriented observers and activists. The issues we will explore will include aspects of international law, transatlantic relations, national security, national sovereignty, NATO, the European Union, development, democratic enhancement on a global scale, environmental challenges, trafficking, treaties, doctrines, agreements, public health, corruption, authoritarian states, human rights including those of minorities, and the role of ngos, pressure groups and constituencies in the formulation of foreign policy.

We will approach international affairs by categories, often overlapping, and subject them to thematic questioning and beliefs. Each of us brings a different set of intellectual and moral formulations and theories to this enquiry. Let me suggest but a few that I think might infuse our discussions: the indefinite boundaries of human rights in international and domestic laws, the mutability of physical borders, the changing nature of governmental and organizational leadership, the role of social media in development and dissent, the contemporary primacy of national identity and loyalty, the right to intervene to thwart aggression, the limits or restraints on intervention, the role of national beliefs and goals in the international realm, the inexplicable tensions between peaceful and violent resolution of differences and the place of retribution in confronting injustice.

And one more category: pluralistic societies. This theme will challenge us throughout the program and distinguish it from others that are important in international issues. Questions about pluralism will intersect with unusual frequency over the next few weeks. This is obvious from the title of the program which has specific goals: to make our societies more effective and constructive in addressing global issues; to increase the long term representation of minorities in the fields of international relations; to recognize power and dignity in diversity based upon different cultural and historical perspectives; to recognize the importance of pluralism as it intersects and sometimes even drives international issues; to expand perspectives in graduate centers to include pluralism in the consideration of international affairs. As we have developed this program, we have discovered that in the United States, at least, pluralism does not exist as a subject in graduate international affairs education. We hope that your participation and the publication of your articles will begin to rectify this situation. Our societies will be strengthened by building on the strengths of those who bring pluralism to the international tables of discourse and power.

This novel educational approach, embodied throughout this program, will constitute a valuable and hopefully exciting exercise in discovery and balance. But it will not be simple. Take, for example, the title of the program: "Diplomacy and Diversity." It has the advantage of alliteration, more importantly it captured your attention as signaling a different kind of study program. But the title lacks subtlety and may be misleading for all that we want to do in dealing with profoundly complex issues. Is Diversity the right word in contemporary nomenclature to define the scope of the program? Is Pluralism a better bet? This is a matter for our ongoing discussions. Beyond the wording, it is important to state at the outset that diversity does not impact or even have primacy in every aspect of international affairs. We will approach subjects in which it plays no part. We also need to be aware that a compelling interest in and experiences of pluralism, which possess powerful intellectual and emotional currents, can sometimes distort issues and inflame discussions.

But it is equally important to recognize that pluralism has often been ignored in ways that impede our efficacious engagement in international affairs, especially by favoring participation by certain groups and excluding others. Thus Humanity in Action has always placed issues of pluralism and democracy at the center of its international mission and pedagogy. Given the complexities of pluralism, it is not surprising that there are enormous tensions and uncertainties in finding resolution with differences in societies—differences that vary deeply from one country or community to another.

Diversity, ipso facto, has the force to be divisive. We can't avoid diversity but we often don't know how to live with it. In some places and societies pluralism is considered desirable based upon religious and political philosophies. Accommodations or adjustments to pluralism are worked out in myriad ways in national contexts that are inextricably connected to national identity. In the most ideal framework, democracy and diversity are intertwined and mutually enriching. A democracy cannot reach its full potential if minorities or majorities are treated unjustly. Of course it is possible to have a democracy in a totally homogeneous society—a rare state of existence that might define paradise for some people. But it is not possible to have a fully democratic state if individuals and groups are denied full rights and opportunities based upon race, religion, color or sexual preference.

Redressing the denial of such rights is one way to address the problems of discrimination, exclusion, powerlessness and victimization. Countless governmental and non-governmental initiatives have made advancements in the representation of minorities in public office, businesses and beyond. These initiatives are exceedingly important and long overdue. Our challenge, in this program and in Humanity in Action as a whole, is somewhat different in conceptual and personal terms. We seek to emphasize that pluralism can be at the root of international tensions and/or domestic tensions that spill into international arenas. Many decades after the Second World War, we now confront another period of intense transformation as issues of pluralism and identity, explosive or potentially explosive, ignite in one country and then reverberate internationally. We are inundated with news of political and religious strife in the Middle East, ethnic, tribal and religious conflicts in Africa and Asia and the growing economic divide between rich and poor in Europe and the United States.

Let us be clear. Today we in America and Western Europe are subject to these same powerful divisive forces. In the fall of 2013, the Tea Party was at the height of its power, seemingly in control of Congress and certainly of the Republican Party. Tea Party activists (and conservatives) shut down the government to drive drastic reductions in federal funding; particularly for certain social programs aimed at improving conditions for underprivileged groups. Other objectives involveds tightening laws against immigrants, particularly illegal immigrants, and delegitimizing the office of the Presidency under America's first black President. After President Lyndon Johnson and his Democratic Party broke the power of segregation in the South, it took just 30 years for the Republican Party to become the dominant political force in the South and Southwestern states. Kill Jim Crow and five decades later we get sequestration, a shutdown and the real possibility of bringing down the international financial system and America's ability to meet its national and international responsibilities.

"In Europe, extremist parties are positioned to gain significant electoral ground in many countries in the next elections. The issues are country specific but the impact transcends national borders in critical ways.

In Europe, extremist parties are positioned to gain significant electoral ground in many countries in the next elections. The issues are country specific but the impact transcends national borders in critical ways. Extremist parties such as Le Pen's in France and Wilders' in the Netherlands are campaigning to tear down certain transnational objectives of the European Union including supranational authenticity and power. Extremists target post war policies that promote human rights, diversity and liberal asylum policies. These campaigns to denigrate and diminish diversity are testing basic ideals that have dominated the Western world since the end of the Second World War.

On both sides of the Atlantic these tensions have deep and chaotic roots in the postwar period—the recovery from the devastation of defeating the Axis powers which had ruled from 1933 to 1945. For 13 years, German Fascists pulverized Europe's democratic structures, established a deathly racial hierarchy and unleashed unprecedented violence on civilian populations. After the defeat of the Nazi state, Western Europe, under the direction of the United States and Great Britain, began its slow march back to civilization. Aggressive nationalism, fueled by racist and ethnic tensions, had to be expiated and contained in the future. The concept of genocide, developed by Raphael Lemkin, gained universal acceptance as did declarations about the primacy of human rights, liberal democratic ideals and structures.

The process of moral recovery, however, was hardly straightforward or politically clean. Democratic ideals and doctrines, restitution on a grand scale and dedication to "never again" were entangled in opposing and contradictory forces. Fighting the Soviet Empire meant employing Nazis in the new German government. Ethnic cleansing and civil wars resulted in massive expulsions in Central and Eastern Europe, the Balkans and Baltics. In the United States, the system of Jim Crow segregation ruled in the South until the Civil Rights movement finally forced the federal government to include African Americans in American democracy and the so-called "American dream." The irony of these developments is the United States triumphed in 1945 in the name of democracy even as it denied its black population its most basic rights and opportunities. At the same time, Europe signed onto pluralism (the ideal or concept thereof) through relatively homogeneous societies in Western Europe and heterogeneous societies in Eastern and Central Europe ruled by dictators and totalitarian regimes.

Thus there is a direct link that ties the decisions and policies of the post-WWII period to the issues and challenges we will be discussing during this program. In developing these thoughts about connecting past to present I have relied heavily upon two historical studies: Keith Lowe's *Savage Continent* and Ira Katznelson's *Fear Itself*. Lowe's book deals with Europe's broken states and the ethnic and national groups that sought, from 1945 to 1949, to rebuild their societies through a toxic mix of new governments, political systems, revenge and violence.

> The immediate postwar period," he writes, "is one of the most important times in our recent history. If the Second World War destroyed the old continent, then its immediate aftermath was the protean chaos out of which the new Europe was formed. It was during this violent, vengeful time that many of our hopes, aspirations, prejudices and resentments first took shape. Anyone who truly wants to understand Europe as it is today must first understand what occurred during this crucial formative period. There is no value in shying away from difficult or sensitive themes, since these are the very building blocks upon which the modern Europe has been built.[38]

Katznelson makes the same claim of causation and continuity in his book *Fear Itself: the New Deal and the Origins of Our Time*. The history of the New Deal,

38 Lowe, Keith, *Savage Continent*, p. 376.

he maintains, should be understood in its global scale. He identifies three major challenges which he maintains were the sources of profound fear that threatened America's democratic system. The first was the fear that liberal democracy in America and Great Britain might not prevail over dictators and totalitarian governments in Germany and the Soviet Union (despite the alliance with Stalin during the war). The second challenge involved building a vast military and security state for fortress America, first against the Axis powers and then to oppose the Russian empire in the hazardous nuclear world. And finally the third challenge: the power of Congressional Southern Democrats who resisted any challenge to segregation in the South. In fighting Germany and then the Soviet Union, Presidents Roosevelt and Truman mobilized the ideology of American democratic ideals and mission. But every international initiative—every one requiring Congressional support—was gained at the price of denying such ideals to the African American population—and not just in the South.

"Placing American developments within a broader global context I ascribe to the New Deal an import almost on a par with that of the French Revolution. It becomes here not merely an important event in the history of the United States but the most important twentieth-century testing ground for representative democracy in an age of mass politics." Katznelson explains further: "Although the United States provided the globe's only major example of a liberal democracy successfully experimenting and resisting radical tyranny, it did not—indeed, could not—remain unaffected by its associations with totalitarian governments or domestic racism."[39]

Keeping in mind the impact of the Second World War and subsequent years of recovery in Europe, and America's reckoning with Jim Crow and continuing discrimination, let us begin to discover and probe the broad and complex intersections of domestic and international policies on current domestic and international actions and objectives. We deeply hope this experiment will deepen your understanding of and strengthen your commitments to expanding diversity in international affairs. We intend to be eclectic in pursuing different topics; we aim to be collaborative in inquiry and output; and we aspire to elevate pluralism to a respected place—well beyond the way it is now perceived and valued—in the conduct of international affairs. All of this in one month! And, finally, we hope to reinforce the words of the great scientist Dr. Jacob Bronokwski who maintained that human knowledge should be gained through a "play of tolerance" guided by the sense that we are engaged in "an unending adventure at the edge of uncertainty."

39 Katznelson, Ira, *Fear Itself: the New Deal and the Origins of Our Time*, p.9.